America's Lost Manners

By Dr. Donita Johnson, D.Min.

Contents

Introduction

In the Bible, God is described in many ways. In the E-sword Bible program you can look up the phrase "God is" and find 150 matches in 149 verses in the King James Version. Many of these are statements of "God is with you," "God is about to do...," "God is upon him...," etc. Looking for God's characteristics you will find the following: God is merciful (Deuteronomy 4:31), God is a jealous God (Deuteronomy 6:15), God is gracious and merciful (Second Chronicles 30:9), God is mighty (Job 36:5), God is great (Job 36:26), God is holy (Psalm 99:9), God is true (John 3:33), God is faithful (First Corinthians 1:9). These are all listed in multiple verses. The one characteristic of God that binds all these together is in 1 John 4:8 and 16, God is love. The Greek word used here is agape (ag-ah'-pay). This is the word used in First Corinthians 13 when Paul said,

> Though I speak with the tongues of men and of angels, and have not charity [love], I am become as sounding brass, or a tinkling cymbal. And though I have the gift of prophecy, and understand all mysteries, and all knowledge; and though I have all faith, so that I could remove mountains, and have not

charity [love], I am nothing. And though I bestow all my goods to feed the poor, and though I give my body to be burned, and have not charity [love], it profiteth me nothing. (First Corinthians 13:1-3)

The apostle tells us how to display this amazing love as followers of Christ. Love is patient and kind. It does not envy or brag. Love is not prideful. It does not behave itself unbecomingly. It is not self-seeking. It is not easily provoked. Love does not keep a record of wrongs. It does not rejoice in iniquity, but rejoices in the truth. It bears all things, believes all things, hopes all things, and endures all things.

I believe there is one characteristic in this list that, if we live by it, all the other characteristics will naturally follow. That is love "doth not behave itself unseemly." (First Corinthians 13:5, KJV) To not behave unseemly is to have good manners. When we have good manners, we treat others with all the other characteristics that describe love here. Today there is no standard of good manners. Everyone is allowed to choose "what is right in his own eyes" with no consequences at all. This is an extreme detriment to society and to our posterity.

It's not just about saying "please," "thank you," and "you're welcome." It is more than just table manners, too. It is having good habits, getting rid of bad habits, and even knowing when good habits can be inappropriate. It is putting others above ourselves and showing proper respect. It is simple common courtesy and common sense.

I once knew a man who picked up every bad habit his friends had. He thought it was funny to watch people's reactions to his bad manners. No one ever told him he was being disrespectful or held him accountable for his bad behavior. Even when people were disgusted, they laughed at him. He saw this as their approval and never saw the need to change. Not only does this excuse bad manners, but it also perpetuates them in children who are watching how we adults respond to ill-mannered people.

We need to teach children the importance of having good manners as well as what those manners should be. In "the old days" in school, children were required to copy down their lessons so that they would remember them better. Though manners have changed since 1744 when George Washington copied his Rules of Civility at twelve years old, it would not hurt at all if we started this practice again. It would be a step forward in getting this "entitled" generation to learn the manners we are failing to teach them.

With that in mind, I have taken Washington's copy work and put it in more modern language. I included Bible verses for most of the rules. For some rules I could find neither verses nor biblical principles.

I have also included an English translation of the French *The RULES of CIVILITY; or, Certain Ways of Deportment observed in France, amongst all Persons of Quality, upon several Occasions* by Antoine de Courtin (1662-1685). This is the book from which many believe Washington copied the rules. I kept most of its original spellings. It also has many footnotes in Latin. Rather than trying to translate them, I have included them as pictures below the paragraphs to which they refer.

At the end of this book I have included a glossary of words that have changed meanings since the 1700's. I have also included words that I felt needed clarified. Though I put the definitions in my own words, the dictionaries used for reference are listed below.

An Universal Etymological English Dictionary by Nathan Bailey (1726)

Dictionarium Britannicum or a More Compleat Universal Etymological English Dictionary Than Any Extant by Nathan Bailey (1730)

The Universal Etymological English Dictionary: Containing An Additional Collection of Words not in the first volume (Bailey's English Dictionary supplementary volume called Volume II, Third edition) (1737)

An Universal Etymological English Dictionary, The Third Edition, with Large Additions by Nathan Bailey (1742)

Rules of Civility

by George Washington

Also called Rules of Civility and Decent Behavior in Company and Conversation

Transcription: Ferry Farm, c. 1744

1. Every action done in company ought to be with some sign of respect to those that are present.

Always be respectful and courteous to everyone. This is the foundational rule of all good manners. We all like to be respected. Jesus said in Matthew 7:12, "Therefore all things whatsoever ye would that men should do to you, do ye even so to them: for this is the Law and the prophets." First Peter 2:17 says, "Honor all men. Love the brotherhood. Fear God. Honor the king." This is the basis of good manners: respect and courtesy toward everyone. We need to teach children to ask themselves, "How would I feel if I were treated that way?"

2. When in company, put not your hands to any part of the body, not usually discovered.

When in public do not touch any part of your body that is not publicly revealed. Be considerate of others and do not embarrass anyone.

3. Show nothing to your friend that may affright him.

Don't purposely try to scare anyone. Proverbs 26:18-19 isn't about scaring a person, but I think it can still apply here. "As a mad man who casteth firebrands, arrows, and death, So is the man that deceiveth his neighbor, and saith, Am not I in sport?" Anytime we seek to deceive, even if it is "only joking," it is not only bad manners, it is sin. Anytime we purposely try to scare anyone, it is deceiving them and leading them to believe that some perceived harm is coming to them. This is still wrong.

4. In the presence of others sing not to yourself with a humming noise, nor drum with your fingers or feet.

When in the presence of others do not sing to yourself or hum. Don't tap your fingers or your feet. Don't be a distraction to others or do anything to draw attention to yourself.

5. If you cough, sneeze, sigh, or yawn, do it not loud, but privately; and speak not in your yawning, but put your handkerchief or hand before your face and turn aside.

If you cough, sneeze, sigh, or yawn, do not draw attention to yourself by making unnecessary noises. Don't try to talk when you yawn. Cover your mouth and turn away from people. In this day of germaphobia we should teach children to use a tissue or their elbows to cover their mouths. Even if it is just allergies and not a cold, we need to consider others' fears and cover our mouths as though it were a cold.

6. Sleep not when others speak, sit not when others stand, speak not when you should hold your peace, walk not on when others stop.

Don't fall asleep when others are speaking. Don't sit when others are standing. Don't speak when you should be quiet. Don't continue walking when others in your group have stopped. Again, this is just being courteous.

7. Put not off your clothes in the presence of others, nor go out of your chamber half dressed.

Don't take off any clothes in the presence of others. Don't come out of your bedroom unless you are fully dressed.

8. At play and at fire it is good manners to give place to the last comer, and affect not to speak louder than ordinary.

Let the last person to come go before you. Do not speak louder than ordinary.

I do not know what it means to be "at fire." I assume he was referring to warming oneself by an open fire or fireplace. Letting the person who came in last go ahead of you is in keeping with Philippians 2:3. "Let nothing be done through strife or vainglory; but in lowliness of mind let each esteem other better than themselves." I really like the Geneva Translation of this verse. "That nothing be done through contention or vain glory, but that in meekness of mind every man esteem others better than himself." It is never acceptable to contentiously put yourself above or ahead of others. It is never acceptable to glorify or raise yourself above others in any way, shape, or form. Be humble. Put others first. "And He [Jesus] sat down, and called the twelve, and saith unto them, If any man desire to be first, the same shall be last of all, and servant of all." (Mark 9:35)

As far as not speaking louder than is ordinary I believe Americans would do well to learn to practice this. I have watched several videos where Europeans compare American manners to their countries' and all of them say American restaurants are too loud. I have also been in restaurants where the group I was with could not carry on a conversation because we could not hear each other even though we were sitting at the same table. Americans seem to have little to no respect for the other parties eating near them and do not keep their conversations at a level where only those at their table can hear them. Everyone speaks as though they are hard of hearing. We have not used this rule of etiquette in decades, but we do need to bring it back into practice and remind others to use it.

9. Spit not in the fire, nor stoop low before it. Neither put your hands into the flames to warm them, nor set your feet upon the fire, especially if there be meat before it.

This rule is pretty straight forward. Don't spit in a fire or stoop in front of it. Don't put your hands into a fire to warm them or put your feet close to the fire, especially if it is being used for cooking.

I'm not sure I understand this rule entirely. I assume it is the idea of not getting in the way of cooking and, probably, not getting in others' way of warming themselves. Put others' comfort before your own. "Let each esteem others better than themselves."

10. When you sit down, keep your feet firm and even, without putting one on the other or crossing them.

Keep your feet flat on the floor. Don't cross your ankles or legs.

It seems our habit of crossing our legs or ankles was considered bad manners in Washington's day. I have heard that it is bad for circulation, so even if it is not bad manners, it is probably healthier to not cross your legs. Teaching our children to take care of their health so that they don't have as many problems in their adult years is also something we need to do. That is not the subject of this book.

11. Shift not yourself in the sight of others nor gnaw your nails.

Don't be fidgety and don't bite your nails.

With the increase of ADD and ADHD, we need to give grace to those who actually have a problem with being fidgety. However, I do believe that too many children are allowed to get by with fidgeting when they should be made to sit still, stand still, etc. They don't have to always be moving. They need to learn not to be a distraction to others, especially in places like church, in theaters, or other public places.

12. Shake not the head, feet, or legs, roll not the eyes, lift not one eyebrow higher than the other, wry not the mouth, and bedew no man's face with your spittle, by approaching too near him [when] you speak.

Don't shake your head, fidget with your feet, roll your eyes, raise your eyebrows, or twist your mouth to one side. Don't get so near to people when speaking that you might accidentally spit on them.

In today's English we would say don't make faces when in conversation, and don't fidget. Don't give them any reason to think you don't care, aren't interested in what they have to say, or that you think they are stupid. The second part of this rule is simple: keep a courteous distance from people and don't spit when you speak.

13. Kill no vermin as fleas, lice, ticks etc. in the sight of others. If you see any filth or thick spittle put your foot dexterously upon it. If it be upon the clothes of your companions, put it off privately, and if it be upon your own clothes, return thanks to him who puts it off.

Don't kill any bugs, insects, or other pests in the sight of others. If you see any filth or thick spittle (i.e. where someone cleared their throat and spat), without drawing attention to it or yourself, put your foot on it. If it is on someone, privately get it off. If someone got it off you, thank that person. This is just simple common courtesy that doesn't draw attention to anything that others might find repulsive or disgusting.

14. Turn not your back to others, especially in speaking. Jog not the table or desk on which another reads or writes. Lean not upon anyone.

Don't turn your back to someone you are speaking to or who is speaking to you. Don't bump a table or desk when someone is reading or writing on it. Don't lean on anyone.

Again, this is just basic courtesy and respect for others. When someone speaks to you, look at them. Pay attention to them. Don't let yourself be distracted. Don't shake a table on which someone is trying to read or write, and I would add, 'or eat.' Don't lean on anyone. Others are not to be unnecessarily used as a support. It shows a lack of respect.

15. Keep your nails clean and short; also your hands and teeth clean yet without showing any great concern for them.

Keep your nails clean and trimmed short. The longer your nails are, the more dirt and bacteria will accumulate under them. It is also more likely that you will accidentally scratch someone and possibly cause an infection if you draw blood.

Keep your hands and teeth clean, but don't show any concern for them when you are in others' company.

16. Do not puff up the cheeks, loll not out the tongue, rub the hands, or beard, thrust out the lips, or bite them or keep the lips too open or too close.

Don't puff up your cheeks, stick out your tongue, rub your hands or beard. Don't puff out your lips, bite them, or keep them too open or too tightly closed.

Sticking out your tongue has long been considered bad manners. This rule sounds like making faces of any kind for any reason was bad manners. I assume it was because it was disrespectful. It also showed that you either weren't paying attention to the conversation or you doubted what was being said. Making the faces described here would be the same as calling the speaker a liar. That is very disrespectful.

17. Be no flatterer, neither play with any that delights not to be played withal.

Avoid all forms of flattery. While everyone likes to get compliments, flattery is complimenting for the purpose of deception or manipulation. Psalm 12:1-3 says, "... Help, LORD; for the godly man ceaseth; for the faithful fail from among the children of men. They speak vanity every one with his neighbor: with flattering lips and with a double heart do they speak. The LORD shall cut off all flattering lips, and the tongue that speaketh proud things."

"To play" in the 1742 English dictionary by Nathan Bailey is, "divertissement." I had to look up that word. In the same dictionary it means, "diversion, recreation, sport, or pastime." Simply put, this rule is: Don't distract anyone who doesn't want to be distracted.

18. Read no letters, books, or papers in company, but when there is a necessity for the doing of it you must ask leave. Come not near the books or writings of another so as to read them unless desired or give your opinion of them unasked. Also look not nigh when another is writing a letter.

Don't read anything when you are with people. Today this would include text messages and email on your cell phone. When you are with someone, your attention needs to be given to their company, not your phone. When there is a necessity, excuse yourself or ask permission. Don't go near another's books or writing to read over their shoulder. If they want you to read it, they will offer it to you. Don't give your opinion unless asked.

Never read over someone's shoulder when they are writing a letter. In today's society this would include texting.

19. Let your countenance be pleasant but in serious matters somewhat grave.

Let your expression be pleasant. In serious matters be composed.

Be a pleasant person, not downcast or depressed all the time. Don't be always joking or laughing, but do be joyful. Be serious when the situation calls for seriousness.

20. The gestures of the body must be suited to the discourse you are upon.

Your gestures and 'body language' must be suited to the subject you are discussing. I think this is probably referring to overreacting to the conversation. Be self-controlled. Self-control or temperance is part of the fruit of the Spirit in Galatians 5:22-23 and a Christian should always exhibit this characteristic.

21. Reproach none for the infirmities of nature, nor delight to put them that have in mind thereof.

Do not disgrace or shame anyone for any type of disability, weakness, or illness. Do not keep bringing it up in conversation or reminding them of it. While we need to be considerate of disabilities and offer help when we can, we need to treat people with the same respect we would if they didn't have a disability.

James chapter two admonishes us against the sin of partiality. While the example he gives is between rich and poor, it can be applied here between able-bodied and disabled. Never treat anyone with any less respect than you would want for yourself.

22. Show not yourself glad at the misfortune of another though he were your enemy.

Don't show gladness at the bad circumstances of another, even if he is your enemy. Proverbs 24:17-18 warns us: "Rejoice not when thine enemy falleth and let not thine heart be glad when he stumbleth: Lest the LORD see it, and it displease Him, and He turn away His wrath from him."

23. When you see a crime punished, you may be inwardly pleased; but always show pity to the suffering offender.

Even if you are pleased when a crime is properly punished, always show compassion to the one being punished.

24. Do not laugh too loud or too much at any public spectacle.

Do not laugh too loud or too much at any public show or sight. Don't draw attention to yourself.

25. Superfluous complements and all affectation of ceremony are to be avoided, yet where due, they are not to be neglected.

Avoid excessive complements and exaggerated formalities or pomp. However, where they are due, they are not to be neglected.

26. In pulling off your hat to persons of distinction, as noblemen, justices, churchmen, etc. make a reverence, bowing more or less according to the custom of the better bred and quality of the person. Amongst your equals expect not always that they should begin with you first, but to pull off the hat when there is no need is affectation. In the manner of saluting and re-saluting in words, keep to the most usual custom.

We no longer live in a society, for the most part, where the rich and well-off are given a higher social class than the middle-income and poor. We don't think about the proper way to greet someone who is richer or poorer than we are. Hopefully we treat everyone as our equals no matter where they are financially. However, in Colonial America such divisions were normal.

When greeting people of distinction, such as noblemen, justices, clergy, etc. remove your hat and reverently bow, according to the custom of the higher social class and title of the person. Among your friends and acquaintances don't expect to be the first to be greeted or shown respect. To take off your hat in a show of respect when there is no need to is pretentious. Keep to usual customs of greeting when meeting anyone.

27. It is ill mannered to bid one more eminent than yourself be covered as well as not to do it to whom it's due. Likewise, he that makes too much haste to put on his hat does not well, yet he ought to put it on at the first, or at most the second time of being asked; now what is herein spoken, of qualification in behavior in saluting, ought also to be observed in taking of place, and sitting down for ceremonies without bounds is troublesome.

It is poor manners to tell your elders or superiors to put on their hats, as well as to not put on your hat when you should. Likewise, he who is in too much of a hurry to put on his hat is ill mannered, yet he ought to put it on the first or second time he is asked. Now what is said here, in qualification of behavior in greeting, ought also to be observed in taking your place and sitting down (with thought to your social status). Ceremonies without limits are disturbing.

I know that in pre-French Revolutionary Europe, there were many rules relating to social hierarchy. However, I have tried without success to find details for Colonial hat etiquette. The above interpretation is my best guess.

28. If anyone comes to speak to you while you are sitting, stand up though he be your inferior, and when you present seats, let it be to everyone according to his degree.

If anyone comes to speak to you while you are sitting, stand up, no matter who he is. When you designate seats, such as at a dinner, let everyone be seated according to his class or station in life. The second half is not done anymore in America since we no longer follow such social class distinctions.

29. When you meet with one of greater quality than yourself, stop, and retire, especially if it be at a door or any straight place to give way for him to pass.

When you meet someone of a higher social status than yourself, stop and step aside, especially if it is at a door or any narrow place to give him room to pass by you.

While social status is not applied in the way it was in the 1700's, it is still courteous to step aside and let others pass through any narrow space first. This is another application of Philippians 2:3, "That nothing be done through contention or vain glory, but that in meekness of mind every man esteem others better than himself." (Geneva Bible)

30. In walking, the highest place in most countries seems to be on the right hand, therefore place yourself on the left of him whom you desire to honor: but if three walk together, the middle place is the most honorable. The wall is usually given to the most worthy if two walk together.

In most countries the place of honor when walking is on the right hand. Therefore, make sure you walk on the left side of someone you desire to honor. However, if you are walking in a group of three, the middle place is the most honorable. The place against the wall [buildings] is usually the honorable place if two are walking together.

While we seldom walk as a mode of travel, I think we would do well to apply this to our manners today when we are walking anywhere. Once again Philippians 2:3 is the most fitting verse to use here.

31. If anyone far surpasses others, either in age, estate, or merit yet would give place to a meaner than himself in his own lodging or elsewhere, the one ought not to accept it, so he on the other part should not use much earnestness nor offer it above once or twice.

If anyone of high status, be it age, social status, or merit, wishes to give his place to someone of lower status, the one of lower status should not accept it. The one of higher status should not insist nor should he offer it more than once or twice.

Again, this is an application of Philippians 2:3 and honoring others above ourselves.

32. To one that is your equal, or not much inferior, you are to give the chief place in your lodging and he to whom it is offered ought at the first to refuse it but at the second to accept, though not without acknowledging his own unworthiness.

To one of your own social status, or not much lower, you should give the best seat in your home. When it is offered, he should first refuse it, but at the second offer should accept it, while acknowledging his own unworthiness.

I think the "first refusing to take it" is for the purpose of knowing your place, so to speak. It is grandiose, even when it is offered, to take a place of honor as though you deserved it somehow. When you are offered a place of honor, you should just say thank you and humbly accept it. You should not act either in false humility or in arrogance. Wisdom speaking in Proverbs 8:13 says, "The fear of the LORD is to hate evil: pride, and arrogancy, and the evil way, and the froward mouth, do I hate." God hates pride and self-exaltation.

33. They that are in dignity or in office have in all places precedence but whilst they are young, they ought to respect those that are their equals in birth or other qualities, though they have no public charge.

Clergy (see second definition of dignity in glossary), dignitaries, and those in positions of authority have precedence everywhere. However, while they are young, they ought to respect those who are their equals in age, rank, etc. even though they hold no public office.

No matter what your position, you should always show respect to those under your authority. You should never "lord it over them." Jesus said in Matthew 20:25-28, "...Ye know that the princes of the Gentiles exercise dominion over them, and they that are great exercise authority upon them. But it shall not be so among you: but whosoever will be great among you, let him be your minister; And whosoever will be chief among you, let him be your servant: Even as the Son of man came not to be ministered unto, but to minister, and to give His life a ransom for many." (See also Mark 10:42-45 and Luke 22:25-27.) In 1 Peter 5:1-3 Peter admonishes the elders. He said, "The elders which are among you I exhort, who am also an elder, and a witness of the sufferings of Christ, and also a partaker of the glory that shall be revealed: Feed the flock of God which is among you, taking the oversight thereof, not by constraint, but willingly; not for filthy lucre, but of a ready mind; Neither as being lords over God's heritage, but being ensamples to the flock."

34. It is good manners to prefer them to whom we speak before ourselves, especially if they be above us with whom in no sort we ought to begin.

It is good manners to esteem above ourselves those to whom we speak, especially if they are socially above us with whom we should speak only when they speak to us.

Esteeming others above ourselves in conversation means to pay attention, put the phone away, and listen. It doesn't matter who they are or what their social status. Give them the same attention you want to be given.

While I abhor the old adage that children "should be seen and not heard," it would be very useful to their future to teach them to listen more, speak less, and never interrupt adults unless it is important or an emergency.

Of course, there is a proper way to interrupt a conversation when it is necessary, yet not an emergency. This they should also be taught. "Excuse me. I'm sorry to interrupt, but..." or some similar proper wording would be a good phrase for them to memorize. When they speak, give them our full attention as we would anyone else.

35. Let your discourse with men of business be short and comprehensive.

When speaking with business associates, your conversation should be short and to the point. You should never take more of their time than is necessary.

You would not want them to monopolize your time when you have things to do.

This brings to my mind Proverbs 10:19, "In the multitude of words there wanteth not sin: but he that refraineth his lips is wise." I like the way the ISV translation puts it: "Transgression is at work where people talk too much, but anyone who holds his tongue is prudent."

36. Artificers and persons of low degree ought not to use many ceremonies to lords, or others of high degree, but respect and highly honor them, and those of high degree ought to treat them with affability and courtesy, without arrogance.

Don't show off or exaggerate your respect for anyone famous or in a position of authority. Simply treat them with respect and honor them as they ought to be honored. Those in a high position or well-known ought to treat others with friendliness and courtesy, and without arrogance.

37. In speaking to men of quality, do not lean nor look them full in the face, nor approach too near them; at least keep a full pace from them.

When speaking to men of title or noble birth, do not lean toward them or look them full in the face. Do not approach too near them. Keep a full pace from them.

I think in today's customs it would be considered ill-mannered and inattentive to not look someone in the eyes but definitely don't lean in toward them. We would say keep them at arm's length. Many people are uncomfortable with someone getting too close to them during conversation. To keep at arm's length is being respectful of that concern, especially if you are not well acquainted.

38. In visiting the sick, do not presently play the physician if you be not knowing therein.

When visiting the sick, don't give medical advice if you are not knowledgeable in their issues.

39. In writing or speaking, give to every person his due title according to his degree and the custom of the place.

In both writing and speaking, refer to each person according to his degree and the customs of the place he lives in.

40. Strive not with your superiors in argument, but always submit your judgment to others with modesty.

Do not argue with those in authority over you or your elders, but humbly submit your opinion to others.

41. Undertake not to teach your equal in the art himself professes; it savors of arrogance.

Don't try to teach anyone in any subject he is proficient in. It is arrogant.

Never assume you know more than someone else. Always show humility. Even when you do have more knowledge in a subject, a person may not be ready for you to teach him. In that case be humble, and if necessary, walk away.

42. Let your ceremonies in courtesy be proper to the dignity of his place with whom you converse, for it is absurd to act the same with a clown and a prince.

Let your show of courtesy be proper to the place of authority or social status of the person with whom you are speaking. It is absurd to use the same manners with a farmer (see Clown in the glossary) and a prince.

Always be aware of where you are and who is with you. Behave appropriately in every situation. Don't act as though a stranger is a close friend. As Solomon said in Ecclesiastes 3:1, "To everything there is a season, and a time to every purpose under the heaven."

43. Do not express joy before one sick or in pain for that contrary passion will aggravate his misery.

Do not express joy in the presence of someone who is experiencing illness, sadness, depression, etc. Your joy will aggravate his troubles. Proverbs 25:20 says, "As he that taketh away a garment in cold weather, and as vinegar upon niter, so is he that singeth songs to an heavy heart." Paul reiterates this in Romans 12:15, "Rejoice with them that do rejoice, and weep with them that weep." In 1 Corinthians 12:26 he said, "And whether one member suffer, all the members suffer with it; or one member be honored, all the members rejoice with it."

44. When a man does all he can, though it succeeds not well, blame not him that did it.

When a man does his best, even though he fails, do not criticize him or blame him for not succeeding.

45. Being to advise or reprehend anyone, consider whether it ought to be in public or in private; presently, or at some other time in what terms to do it and in reproving show no sign of choler but do it with all sweetness and mildness.

When advising or reproving anyone, consider whether it should be in public or in private. Consider also whether it needs to be done now or if it can wait. Consider your words as well and do not show signs of anger, but do it with kindness and gentleness.

Jesus addressed this in Matthew 18:15-17. "Moreover if thy brother shall trespass against thee, go and tell him his fault between thee and him alone: if he shall hear thee, thou hast gained thy brother. But if he will not hear thee, then take with thee one or two more, that in the mouth of two or three witnesses every word may be established. And if he shall neglect to hear them, tell it unto the church: but if he neglect to hear the church, let him be unto thee as an heathen man and a publican." Do not unnecessarily humiliate anyone in public. Don't address an issue publicly if it is not something the public knows about. I think Ecclesiastes 3 can also be applied here. If it is not the right time or the right place, wait for a better time and place.

46. Take all admonitions thankfully in what time or place soever given but afterwards, not being culpable, take a time and place convenient to let him know it that gave them.

Take all correction thankfully whenever and wherever given. If you are not guilty of the accusation, privately go to the one who corrected you and explain the situation.

47. Mock not nor jest at anything of importance. Break no jests that are sharp biting, and if you deliver anything witty and pleasant, abstain from laughing thereat yourself.

Do not mock or joke about any important or serious matter. Do not joke in any insulting or hurtful manner. "As a mad man who casteth firebrands, arrows, and death, So is the man that deceiveth his neighbor, and saith, Am not I in sport?" (Proverbs 26:18-19). "Let no corrupt communication proceed out of your mouth, but that which is good to the use of edifying, that it may minister grace unto the hearers." (Ephesians 4:29). If you tell a joke or say anything witty, don't laugh at yourself.

48. Wherein you reprove another be unblameable yourself; for example is more prevalent than precepts.

In whatever matter you reprove someone, don't be guilty of it yourself. Example is more effective than commands.

That is not to say that if you repented and learned from your mistakes, that you can't warn or reprove anyone who is making those same mistakes. If you have not repented, it is best not to try to correct someone when you can't or won't correct yourself.

49. Use no reproachful language against anyone; neither curse nor revile.

Do not use abusive or shameful language against anyone. Do not wish ill on, taunt, or use harsh, offensive words toward anyone.

50. Be not hasty to believe flying reports to the disparagement of any.

Do not be quick to believe gossip or contemptuous reports of anyone.

There are several verses about talebearers and gossip. Leviticus 19:16 is the command, "Thou shalt not go up and down as a talebearer among thy people." Proverbs 18:8 and 26:22 say, "The words of a talebearer are as wounds, and they go down into the innermost parts of the belly." Some Bible version translate "wounds" as "choice morsels" but this is a poor translation in my opinion. The Hebrew word is lah-hahm' and Strong's Hebrew Dictionary defines it as, "to burn or rankle." To rankle is to fester. Choice morsels don't fester. Gossip is a wound that goes deep into a person's spirit and festers. Proverbs 18:19 says, "A brother offended is harder to be won than a strong city: and their contentions are like the bars of a castle." It is better to stop a gossiper from speaking than to have to win back a friend you offended by not doing so.

51. Wear not your clothes, foul, unripped or dusty but see they be brushed once every day at least and take heed that you approach not to any uncleanness.

Don't wear dirty, ripped, or dusty clothes. Brush them at least once a day and don't go near any filthiness.

In Colonial days laundry was hard work and an all-day chore. Most people made their own lye soap which was hard on hands and clothing alike. People would brush their clothes between washings, so they didn't have to be washed as often.

As we have seen in the previous rules, we should present ourselves in a way that does not offend anyone's sense of propriety or offend in any way. This includes the senses of sight, smell, touch, and hearing.

"Cleanliness is next to godliness" is not found in the Bible. That being said, the principle is there. Uncleanness is symbolic of sin. Anyone who was unclean had to stay outside of the camp or village. In Leviticus 13:46 a leper had to live alone outside the camp. Deuteronomy 23:10 says that anyone who somehow became unclean at night had to go outside the camp until evening. After he washed himself then he could come back in.

Many places in the Bible talk of changing filthy garments for clean ones. In Zechariah chapter 3 the Lord showed Zechariah a vision of Joshua the high priest dressed in filthy garments that symbolized sin. God told those that stood before Him to take away the filthy garments from Joshua. God then told Joshua he was forgiven and gave him a change of clothes and set a crown on his head.

> Now Joshua was clothed with filthy garments, and stood before the angel. And he answered and spake unto those that stood before him, saying, Take away the filthy garments from him. And unto him he said, Behold, I have caused thine

iniquity to pass from thee, and I will clothe thee with change of raiment. And I said, Let them set a fair miter upon his head. So they set a fair miter upon his head, and clothed him with garments. And the angel of the LORD stood by. Zechariah 3:3-5

First Thessalonians 4:7 makes the simple statement that God has not called us unto uncleanness, but unto holiness.

James tells us to cleanse our hands and purify our hearts.

Draw nigh to God, and he will draw nigh to you. Cleanse your hands, ye sinners; and purify your hearts, ye double minded. James 4:8

Taking our cues from Scripture, we should always wear clean clothes that are in good condition.

52. In your apparel be modest and endeavor to accommodate nature. Rather than to procure admiration, keep to the fashion of your equals such as are civil and orderly with respect to times and places.

In your dress, be modest, discreet, and self-controlled. Don't dress to attract attention or gain praise. Be considerate of others and dress in an orderly and disciplined fashion. Keep in mind what you will be doing and where you will be going.

Clothing that "accommodates nature" fits correctly and covers that which no one needs to see. In other words, don't wear revealing or form-fitting clothes.

In the 1742 English dictionary by Nathan Bailey, to admire is "to look upon with wonder, to be surprised at." By this definition admiration may not always be a good thing. The Bible says in 1 Timothy 2:9, "...that women adorn themselves in modest apparel, with shamefacedness and sobriety; not with broided hair, or gold, or pearls, or costly array." Shamefaced simply means modest or bashful. Sobriety is self-control and moderation. Our clothes are not to draw attention to ourselves, our finances, or anything else. Clothing is not for "keeping up with the Jones'." We should "keep to the fashion of our equals." We shouldn't try to dress like we are richer than we are, nor should we dress to show off our riches when we are among those who don't have the finances we are blessed with.

53. Run not in the streets, neither go too slowly nor with mouth open. Go not shaking your arms. Kick not the earth with your feet, go not upon the toes, nor in a dancing fashion.

Don't run in the streets. Don't go too slowly or with your mouth open. Don't shake your arms or kick the earth. Don't walk on your toes or in a dancing manner.

This is probably to keep from endangering yourself or others. Kicking up dust that would get dirt on others' clothes would make it necessary for them to wash their clothes more than they usually would. In other words, don't make unnecessary work for others and don't be a danger to anyone. It could also apply to not drawing attention to yourself.

54. Play not the peacock, looking everywhere about you, to see if you be well decked, if your shoes fit well if your stockings sit neatly, and clothes handsomely.

Don't be a show-off or always looking at yourself to make sure your clothes are well-fitting and in place.

55. Eat not in the streets, nor in the house, out of season.

Don't eat in the streets or in the house when it's not a set time to be eating.

Could this be one reason obesity is so rampant in our society? Food is readily available at all hours of the day. Whenever our appetite – not true hunger – tells us to eat, we can grab a burger or whatever we want. We don't have to control ourselves and wait for our next meal. Since we basically have a 24-7 lifestyle that will not change, we need to apply the God-given self-control we have. We need to discipline ourselves, not give in to our appetites or the ads that appeal to them. Overeating is simply a less offensive word for gluttony. Gluttony is sin and it leads to obesity. God expects us to be self-controlled. "But the fruit of the Spirit is love, joy, peace, longsuffering, gentleness, goodness, faith, Meekness, temperance: against such there is no law." (Galatians 5:22-23) God has given us everything we need (2nd Peter 1:3) to live lives that glorify Him. Maybe applying good manners to our appetite, i.e. not eating when it's not time to eat, would help us overcome the sin of gluttony.

56. Associate yourself with men of good quality if you esteem your own reputation; for 'tis better to be alone than in bad company.

If you value your reputation, choose friends who are of high morals. It is better to be alone than in bad company.

The Bible has a lot to say about associating with people who have poor morals and no character. Here are just a few verses.

"He that walketh with wise men shall be wise: but a companion of fools shall be destroyed." (Proverbs 13:20)

"Go from the presence of a foolish man, when thou perceivest not in him the lips of knowledge." (Proverbs 14:7)

"Whoso keepeth the law is a wise son: but he that is a companion of riotous men shameth his father." (Proverbs 28:7)

"Be not deceived: evil communications corrupt good manners." (1 Corinthians 15:33)

57. In walking up and down in a house, only with one in company if he be greater than yourself, at the first give him the right hand and stop not till he does and be not the first that turns, and when you do turn let it be with your face towards him. If he be a man of great quality, walk not with him cheek by jowl but somewhat behind him; but yet in such a manner that he may easily speak to you.

When walking inside a house with a person, if he is of a higher status than yourself, walk to his left. Don't stop unless he does, and don't be the first to turn into a room walking away while he is still talking. When you need to turn into a room, turn towards him and give him time to end the conversation before walking away. If he is a man of high status, don't walk shoulder to shoulder. Walk slightly behind him; yet not too far behind that he may easily speak to you.

58. Let your conversation be without malice or envy, for 'tis a sign of a tractable and commendable nature. And in all causes of passion admit reason to govern.

Let your conversation be without spite or jealousy. This shows a gentle, self-controlled, and admirable character. In all causes of temper or anger, be sensible and self-controlled.

My favorite Bible verse about the words we say is Ephesians 4:29. "Let no corrupt communication proceed out of your mouth, but that which is good to the use of edifying, that it may minister grace unto the hearers." When we refuse to "vent" about jealousies or perceived wrongs, we display self-control. When we control our words and our attitudes, we exhibit gentleness and an admirable character.

There are many verses about anger. Some that reiterate controlling our temper are these.

Psalms 37:8 "Cease from anger, and forsake wrath: fret not thyself in any wise to do evil.

Proverbs 19:11 The discretion of a man deferreth his anger; and it is his glory to pass over a transgression.

Colossians 3:8 But now ye also put off all these; anger, wrath, malice, blasphemy, filthy communication out of your mouth.

James 1:19-20 Wherefore, my beloved brethren, let every man be swift to hear, slow to speak, slow to wrath: For the wrath of man worketh not the righteousness of God.

59. Never express anything unbecoming, nor act against the rules moral before your inferiors.

Never say anything indecent nor act against the rules of morality before your inferiors.

While there are hundreds of verses about the use of our words, I will list only one here.

"Let no corrupt communication proceed out of your mouth, but that which is good to the use of edifying, that it may minister grace unto the hearers." (Ephesians 4:29)

60. Be not immodest in urging your friends to discover a secret.

Don't try to force your friends to reveal a secret.

"Debate thy cause with thy neighbor himself; and discover not a secret to another." (Proverbs 25:9)

"A talebearer revealeth secrets: but he that is of a faithful spirit concealeth the matter." (Proverbs 11:13)

"He that goeth about as a talebearer revealeth secrets: therefore, meddle not with him that flattereth with his lips." (Proverbs 20:19)

Pushing someone to reveal a secret is asking them to betray a trust. We would not want someone to share something that we told them in confidence. We should not ask anyone to do what we would not have done to us. We should help them keep their secret by not asking them to reveal it.

"Therefore all things whatsoever ye would that men should do to you, do ye even so to them: for this is the law and the prophets." (Matthew 7:12)

61. Utter not base and frivolous things amongst grave and learned men nor very difficult questions or subjects among the ignorant, or things hard to be believed. Stuff not your discourse with sentences amongst your betters nor equals.

Do not say anything vile, cowardly, or dishonest among serious and educated men. Don't talk with them about frivolous things that are of no value or are vain or foolish. Don't discuss difficult questions or subjects, or things hard to believe, among those who do not have knowledge of those things. Do not fill your conversations with unnecessary sentences among your superiors or equals. Don't be wordy or filibuster. Don't try to make yourself look educated or smarter than those you are talking with. Be humble.

"Humble yourselves in the sight of the Lord, and He shall lift you up." (James 4:10)

62. Speak not of doleful things in a time of mirth or at the table. Speak not of melancholy things as death and wounds, and if others mention them, change if you can the discourse. Tell not your dreams, but to your intimate friend.

Don't speak of sad or mournful things in a time of happiness or at the table. Don't speak of sad things as death and injuries. If others mention them, change the subject if you can. Don't tell your dreams to anyone but your closest friend.

63. A man ought not to value himself of his achievements, or rare qualities of wit, much less of his riches, virtue, or kindred.

No one should be too prideful or over-value himself for his achievements or wittiness; much less of his wealth, authority, genealogy or family connections.

64. Break not a jest where none take pleasure in mirth. Laugh not aloud, nor at all without occasion. Deride no man's misfortune, though there seem to be some cause.

Don't make jokes when it is inappropriate. Don't mock or laugh at anyone's misery or disasters, even if it seems deserved.

This is not only poor manners; it is displeasing to God.

"Rejoice not when thine enemy falleth, and let not thine heart be glad when he stumbleth: Lest the LORD see it, and it displease Him, and he turn away his wrath from him." (Proverbs 24:17-18)

65. Speak not injurious words, neither in jest nor earnest; scoff at none although they give occasion.

Don't say hurtful things. Don't mock anyone, either jokingly or seriously, even if they give you a reason.

Solomon had a lot to say in Proverbs about our words.

"There is that speaketh like the piercings of a sword: but the tongue of the wise is health." (Proverbs 12:18)

"A man that beareth false witness against his neighbor is a maul, and a sword, and a sharp arrow." (Proverbs 25:18)

"As a mad man who casteth firebrands, arrows, and death, So is the man that deceiveth his neighbor, and saith, 'Am not I in sport?'" (Proverbs 26:18-19)

It is never okay to hurt someone as a joke, whether it is deceiving them or saying something that you know will hurt them. Jokes, or any kind of "humor," that hurts is not funny. If you truly love your neighbor as yourself, you would not do or say anything that would hurt him.

Jesus gave us a warning about our words. "A good man out of the good treasure of the heart bringeth forth good things: and an evil man out of the evil treasure bringeth forth evil things. But I say unto you, That every idle word that men shall speak, they shall give account thereof in the day of judgment." (Matthew 12:35-36) We will give an account of our words when we stand before God. Use your words wisely and consider that you will be judged for what you say. The next verse in Matthew says, "For by thy words thou shalt be justified, and by thy words thou shalt be condemned." (Matthew 12:37)

66. Be not froward but friendly and courteous; the first to salute, hear and answer and be not pensive when it's a time to converse.

Don't be easily irritated or ill tempered. Be friendly and courteous. Be the first to greet someone respectfully. Listen and answer readily. Don't be lost in thought when it's time to speak.

James 1:19 says, "Wherefore, my beloved brethren, let every man be swift to hear, slow to speak, slow to wrath." Another verse that fits with this rule is Proverbs 14:29, "He that is slow to wrath is of great understanding: but he that is hasty of spirit exalteth folly." First Corinthians 13:5 applies as well, "[Love] Doth not behave itself unseemly, seeketh not her own, is not easily provoked, thinketh no evil."

67. Detract not from others, neither be excessive in commanding.

Do not lessen the value of others; either their input in a conversation or their value as a person. Don't be domineering or always commanding others.

Someone who is living out God's agape love values others and their input. They don't need to be the center of attention.

68. Go not thither, where you know not, whether you shall be welcome or not. Give not advice without being asked and when desired do it briefly.

Don't go anywhere where you do not know if you will be welcomed or not. Don't give unsolicited advice. When your advice is asked for, give it briefly; not long drawn out explanations.

If you know you will be welcomed, it's acceptable to go visiting. In the days before telephones, texting, or internet, neighbors often visited each other without prior notice. However, Proverbs 25:17 also warns us not to make a nuisance of ourselves, "Withdraw thy foot from thy neighbor's house; lest he be weary of thee, and so hate thee."

69. If two contend together, take not the part of either unconstrained; and be not obstinate in your own opinion. In things indifferent, be of the major side.

Don't take part in an argument that is not your own. Don't be opinionated. In matters of little importance take the side of the majority.

Proverbs 26:17 says, "He that passeth by, and meddleth with strife belonging not to him, is like one that taketh a dog by the ears." The Septuagint of this verse translates it "as he that holdeth the tail of a dog." If you either grab a dog by the ears or hold its tail, you put yourself in danger of being bitten, especially if the dog is already angry. It is the same when you get involved in an argument that is none of your business. You put yourself in danger of being attacked by one or both parties in the argument.

Obstinacy is "a stubborn resolve to do anything right or wrong; a fixedness in maintaining an opinion;

willfulness." An obstinate person is unteachable and won't listen to advice. Proverbs 18:2 says, "A fool has no delight in understanding, But in expressing his own heart." Being stubborn and opinionated is foolish and prideful. The book of Proverbs has many warnings about being prideful.

> "When pride cometh, then cometh shame: but with the lowly is wisdom." (Proverbs 11:2)

> "Pride goeth before destruction, and an haughty spirit before a fall." (Proverbs 16:18)

> "Before destruction the heart of man is haughty, and before honor is humility." (Proverbs 18:12)

The last part of this rule seems to be about not being divisive. Don't be one who argues just to argue. Proverbs 17:19 says, "He loveth transgression that loveth strife: and he that exalteth his gate seeketh destruction." A love of arguing is sin.

70. Reprehend not the imperfections of others for that belongs to parents, masters, and superiors.

Do not rebuke others for their shortcomings. That responsibility belongs to parents, masters, and superiors.

There are times when it is better to put up with someone's "imperfections" or lack of manners. At those times we should be kind and helpful to the person who is lacking. If we cannot guide them without embarrassing them, we should cover for them when necessary and talk to them or to their parents or superiors later. To be rude to them because of their shortcomings is just as bad as their not displaying proper manners.

The first verse that I thought of for this rule was Romans 14:4, "Who art thou that judgest another man's servant? To his own master he standeth or falleth. Yea, he shall be holden up: for God is able to make him stand." The second verse was Galatians 6:1, "Brethren, if a man be overtaken in a fault, ye which are spiritual, restore such an one in the spirit of meekness; considering thyself, lest thou also be tempted." Usually we should not correct a person's poor manners in public. When we do correct them, we should do so privately and remember that it could be us in their place.

71. Gaze not on the marks or blemishes of others and ask not how they came. What you may speak in secret to your friend deliver not before others.

Don't stare at others' birthmarks, scars, etc. and don't ask what happened to the person who has them. Don't speak of personal matters in public.

Staring makes people uncomfortable. It makes them feel self-conscious. It has long been considered poor manners to stare for any reason. Someone who has a "mark or blemish" does not need to be reminded or asked about the situation that gave them that mark. It may be traumatic for them. Matthew 7:12 and Philippians 2:3 both suggest that if we don't want asked about our scars, we shouldn't ask others about theirs.

Knowing when to keep your mouth shut requires discretion. Proverbs 1:4 tells us Solomon's proverbs were written down "to give subtility to the simple, to the young man knowledge and discretion." In Proverbs 17:27-28 we are told, "He that hath knowledge spareth his words: and a man of understanding is of an excellent spirit. Even a fool, when he holdeth his peace, is counted wise: and he that shutteth his lips is esteemed a man of understanding."

72. Speak not in an unknown tongue in company but in your own language and that as those of quality do and not as the vulgar. Sublime matters treat seriously.

Don't speak in a foreign language among people who don't speak that same language. Be polite in your speech. Don't use vulgar language. Treat serious matters seriously.

While Paul is speaking of gifts used in the church setting in 1 Corinthians 14, his admonition to edify the group is practicing good manners. There is nothing praiseworthy in speaking a language no one understands to prove that you can. When we are in a multi-lingual group, it is rude to speak in a language one person doesn't understand. It is the same as whispering to keep them from hearing or understanding what is being said.

73. Think before you speak. Pronounce not imperfectly nor bring out your words too hastily but orderly and distinctly.

Think before you speak. Pronounce words correctly. Don't speak too quickly, but enunciate properly and clearly.

The purpose of words is to clearly communicate our thoughts, ideas, and, more importantly, the Gospel to those God has put in our lives. If we do not use wisdom in our word choices, we may offend someone or we may be misunderstood. They may think we are simple minded idiots. We should take care that we speak wisely and clearly. We should also keep these verses in mind:

"To everything there is a season, and a time to every purpose under the heaven: ... a time to rend, and a time to sew; a time to keep silence, and a time to speak..." (Ecclesiastes 3:1 and 7)

"A fool uttereth all his mind: but a wise man keepeth it in till afterwards." (Proverbs 29:11)

"Seest thou a man that is hasty in his words? there is more hope of a fool than of him." (Proverbs 29:20)

"A word fitly spoken is like apples of gold in pictures of silver." (Proverbs 25:11)

74. When another speaks, be attentive yourself and disturb not the audience. If anyone hesitates in his words, help him not nor prompt him without desired, interrupt him not, nor answer him till his speech be ended.

When another speaks, pay attention. Don't disturb other listeners. If anyone hesitates in his words, don't help him or prompt him unless he asks. Don't interrupt him or answer him until he is finished speaking.

I do not know of a Bible verse that specifically answers this rule. Proverbs 18:13 says, "He that answereth a matter before he heareth it, it is folly and shame unto him." The apocryphal book of Sirach, chapter 11, verse 8, says, "Answer not before thou hast heard the cause: neither interrupt men in the midst of their talk." Close friends often know each other well enough to finish each other's sentences. We should be careful not to offer unwanted help. Sometimes it can be frustrating to the speaker if we are wrong in assuming we know what they are thinking. While it may not be considered bad manners today; it used to be, and may still be, in some circles.

75. In the midst of discourse ask not of what one treats, but if you perceive any stop because of your coming, you may well intreat him gently to proceed. If a person of quality comes in while you are conversing, it's handsome to repeat what was said before.

If you walk into the middle of a conversation, don't ask what they are talking about. If you see that the conversation stopped because of your coming, you may ask the speaker to continue. If a person of high standing comes in while you are conversing, it is good manners to repeat what was said before.

This is simply a rule of not forcing your way into a conversation, not making yourself the center of attention, and not letting another person be (or feel that they are) left out. Just be nice and considerate of others.

76. While you are talking, point not with your finger at him of whom you discourse nor approach too near him to whom you talk, especially to his face.

Don't point at the person you are talking about. Don't get in the face of the person you are talking to.

Everyone has their own "personal space." It varies person to person. If someone keeps backing away, give them space.

77. Treat with men at fit times about business and whisper not in the company of others.

Bargain with men at suitable times about business. Don't whisper in the company of others.

Doing business or bargaining is not in this list but Ecclesiastes 3:1-8 says there is a fit time for everything.

> To everything there is a season, and a time to every purpose under the heaven: A time to be born, and a time to die; a time to plant, and a time to pluck up that which is planted; A time to kill, and a time to heal; a time to break down, and a time to build up; A time to weep, and a time to laugh; a time to mourn, and a time to dance; A time to cast away stones, and a time to gather stones together; a time to embrace, and a time to refrain from embracing; A time to get, and a time to lose; a time to keep, and a time to cast away; A time to rend, and a time to sew; a time to keep silence, and

a time to speak; A time to love, and a time to hate; a time of war, and a time of peace.

There is no Bible verse that says, "Thou shalt not whisper." Proverbs 16:28 says, "A froward man soweth strife: and a whisperer separateth chief friends." Psalm 41:7 implies that whispering is done by those who hate the one they are whispering about. "All that hate me whisper together against me: against me do they devise my hurt."

78. Make no comparisons and if any of the company be commended for any brave act of virtue, commend not another for the same.

Don't compare anyone to another person. If anyone in your company is commended for any brave act of virtue, don't commend anyone else for the same act.

Making comparisons between people is more about lifting ourselves up — or sometimes putting ourselves down — than learning to make ourselves better. It's more about pleasing men than pleasing God. Humility is a foundational characteristic of mature Christians. Humility helps others instead of comparing. In his farewell to the Ephesian elders, Paul said, "I have shewed you all things, how that so laboring ye ought to support the weak, and to remember the words of the Lord Jesus, how he said, It is more blessed to give than to receive." (Acts 20:35) We should support the weak and give them the help they need. Romans 12:3 commands humility. "For I say, through the grace given unto me, to every man that is among you, not to think of himself more highly than he ought to think; but to think soberly, according as God hath dealt to every man the measure of faith." A favorite of mine is 1 Corinthians 4:7, "For who maketh thee to differ from another? and what hast thou that thou didst not receive? now if thou didst receive it, why dost thou glory, as if thou hadst not received it?" Paul is asking, "Who do you think you are?" Everything we have and are comes from God. (Every good gift and every perfect gift is from above, and cometh down from the Father of lights, with whom is no variableness, neither shadow of turning. James 1:17) There is no reason for us to either look down on others or look down on ourselves.

79. Be not apt to relate news if you know not the truth thereof. In discoursing of things you have heard, name not your author. Always a secret discover not.

Don't be quick to relate news if you don't know its validity. In discussing things you have heard, don't name who told you. Never reveal a secret.

If you don't know the validity of something, yet state it as a fact, you could be guilty of unintentionally lying. God hates lying. Proverbs 6:16-19 lists lying among seven things that are an abomination to Him.

Proverbs 25:9 says, "Debate thy cause with thy neighbor himself; and discover not a secret to another." To reveal a secret is to betray the trust someone has placed in you. The Old Testament uses the word "talebearer" to describe one who won't keep secrets. Proverbs 11:13 says, "A talebearer revealeth secrets: but he that is of a faithful spirit concealeth the matter." Proverbs 18:8 and 26:22 say, "The words of a talebearer are as wounds, and they go down into the innermost parts of the belly." Revealing a secret is like stabbing someone in the gut. It is the death of a friendship. While forgiveness and restoration are possible, the friendship will never be the same.

80. Be not tedious in discourse or in reading unless you find the company pleased therewith.

Don't be long-winded in talking or in reading out loud unless you find your company is pleased to listen to it.

Two verses, both from Solomon, speak of talking too much. Proverbs 10:19 says, "In the multitude of words there wanteth not sin: but he that refraineth his lips is wise." In my E-sword program I have the Apostolic Bible Polyglot. It translates this verse this way: "By many words you shall not flee from sin; but in the sparing of your lips you will be intelligent." The International Standard Version (ISV) says, "Transgression is at work where people talk too much, but anyone who holds his tongue is prudent." It is intelligent and wise to know when to shut up.

The second verse is Ecclesiastes 5:3, "For a dream cometh through the multitude of business; and a fool's voice is known by multitude of words." I like the ISV's wording: "Too many worries lead to nightmares, and a fool is known from talking too much." If you don't want to be considered a fool, know how and when to condense your words.

81. Be not curious to know the affairs of others, neither approach those that speak in private.

Don't be nosy. Don't approach those who are in a private conversation.

In 1 Thessalonians we are commanded to live a quiet life, mind our own business, and work with our own hands. "And that ye study to be quiet, and to do your own business, and to work with your own hands, as we commanded you." (1 Thessalonians 4:11) A nosy person is a busybody and that often leads to gossip. The Bible calls both sin.

82. Undertake not what you cannot perform but be careful to keep your promise.

Don't try to do what you know you cannot perform but be careful to keep your promises.

There are times when breaking a promise can't be helped. It is then we need to apologize and do our best to make it up to the person. Psalm 15 asks the question, "Lord, who shall abide in Thy tabernacle?" The list of answers includes speaking truth to yourself and keeping your word even when it hurts.

> LORD, who shall abide in Thy tabernacle? who shall dwell in Thy holy hill? He that walketh uprightly, and worketh righteousness, and speaketh the truth in his heart. He that backbiteth not with his tongue, nor doeth evil to his neighbor, nor taketh up a reproach against his neighbor. In whose eyes a vile person is contemned; but he honoreth them that fear the LORD. He that

sweareth to his own hurt, and changeth not. He that putteth not out his money to usury, nor taketh reward against the innocent. He that doeth these things shall never be moved. (Psalms 15:1-5)

In Matthew 5:33 37 and in James 5:12 we are commanded to not make oaths or swear, but simply let our "yes" be "yes," and our "no" be "no." Just answer "yes" or "no" and keep your word. It's called integrity.

83. When you deliver a matter, do it without passion and with discretion, however mean the person be you do it to.

When you deliver a message, do it without anger and with wisdom, regardless of the behavior of the person to whom you are delivering it.

First Thessalonians 5:15 commands, "See that none render evil for evil unto any man; but ever follow that which is good, both among yourselves, and to all men." Another verse that can apply here is Romans 12:19, "Dearly beloved, avenge not yourselves, but rather give place unto wrath: for it is written, Vengeance is mine; I will repay, saith the Lord." It's not our job to get back at someone for their ungodly behavior. It's God's job. Furthermore, when we are delivering a message, it is more for the benefit of the sender than the receiver. Proverbs 25:13 says, "As the cold of snow in the time of harvest, so is a faithful messenger to them that send him: for he refresheth the soul of his masters." It is better to be a faithful messenger than to concern ourselves with correcting someone's behavior for whom we are not responsible.

84. When your superiors talk to anybody, hearken not, neither speak nor laugh.

When your superiors talk to anybody, don't eavesdrop, don't enter the conversation, and don't laugh.

Stay out of business that isn't yours. Ecclesiastes 7:21 says, "Also take no heed unto all words that are spoken lest thou hear thy servant curse thee." If you have a habit of eavesdropping, you may hear things you'll wish you hadn't.

85. In company of those of higher quality than yourself, speak not till you are asked a question; then stand upright, put off your hat, and answer in few words.

When in the company of your elders or superiors, don't speak until you are asked a question. At that time stand up, take off your hat, and answer in as few words as possible. Don't be "wordy" and stick to the subject of the question you were asked.

When you are in a group who seem to be more knowledgeable about a subject, it is proper to keep quiet until you are asked a question. Sometimes it is better to listen and learn.

There are many verses that could apply to "answering in a few words."

> "In the multitude of words there wanteth not sin: but he that refraineth his lips is wise." (Proverbs 10:19)

"He that hath knowledge spareth his words: and a man of understanding is of an excellent spirit." (Proverbs 17:27)

"Whoso keepeth his mouth and his tongue keepeth his soul from troubles." (Proverbs 21:23)

"For in the multitude of dreams and many words there are also divers vanities: but fear thou God." (Ecclesiastes 5:7)

"Wherefore, my beloved brethren, let every man be swift to hear, slow to speak, slow to wrath." (James 1:19)

It is annoying to the listeners when someone has to explain every detail of their answer and go off on innumerable rabbit trails when a simple yes or no will suffice. When more than yes or no is necessary, remember that all the details don't need to be described.

86. In disputes, be not so desirous to overcome as not to give liberty to each one to deliver his opinion and submit to the judgment of the major part, especially if they are judges of the dispute.

In disagreements or arguments, don't be so desirous of winning that you don't let everyone express their opinions. Be willing to surrender to the ruling of the majority, especially if they are set as judges of the dispute.

Be humble. It's not about you. You don't have to be proven right even if you are right.

"Likewise, ye younger, submit yourselves unto the elder. Yea, all of you be subject one to another, and be clothed with humility: for God resisteth the proud, and giveth grace to the humble. Humble yourselves therefore under the mighty hand of God, that he may exalt you in due time." (1 Peter 5:5-6)

87. Let thy carriage be such as becomes a man: grave, settled, and attentive to that which is spoken. Contradict not at every turn what others say.

Let your behavior be such as is becoming to a man: composed, serious, fixed in place and mind, and attentive to what is spoken. Don't constantly contradict what others say.

One biblical word for behavior is "conversation." Here are a few verses about proper "conversation."

> "Whoso offereth praise glorifieth Me: and to him that ordereth his conversation aright will I shew the salvation of God." (Psalms 50:23)

> "But ye have not so learned Christ; If so be that ye have heard Him, and have been taught by Him, as the truth is in Jesus: That ye put off concerning the former conversation the old man, which is corrupt according to the deceitful lusts; And be renewed in the spirit of your mind; And that ye put on the new

man, which after God is created in righteousness and true holiness." (Ephesians 4:20-24)

"Only let your conversation be as it becometh the gospel of Christ: that whether I come and see you, or else be absent, I may hear of your affairs, that ye stand fast in one spirit, with one mind striving together for the faith of the gospel." (Philippians 1:27)

"Let no man despise thy youth; but be thou an example of the believers, in word, in conversation, in charity, in spirit, in faith, in purity." (1 Timothy 4:12)

"Let your conversation be without covetousness; and be content with such things as ye have: for he hath said, I will never leave thee, nor forsake thee." (Hebrews 13:5)

"Who is a wise man and endued with knowledge among you? let him shew out of a good conversation his works with meekness of wisdom." (James 3:13)

"But as he which hath called you is holy, so be ye holy in all manner of conversation; Because it is written, Be ye holy; for I am holy." (1 Peter 1:15-16)

Constantly contradicting what others say is more likely to start an argument than correct an error. Second Timothy 2:24 says, "And the servant of the Lord must not strive, but be gentle unto all men."

88. Be not tedious in discourse, make not many digressions, nor repeat often the same manner of discourse.

Don't be long-winded. Stick to the subject you're talking about. Don't be repetitive.

Being long winded is wasting words as well as wasting time. When Job was answering what his friends said to him, he asked, "Will windy words like yours never end? What is upsetting you that you keep on arguing?" (Job 16:3 ISV). The scribes and Pharisees made long, wordy prayers for show (Matthew 23:14). Jesus commanded us in Matthew 6:7 not to pray with useless repetitions as the heathen did, "for they think that they shall be heard for their much speaking." Tedious, repetitive wordiness indicates either a lack of clear thinking or a desire to gain the praise of men. Whether it is in prayer or in common conversation, it is inconsiderate and annoying. It was ill-mannered in George Washington's day and it still is.

89. Speak not evil of the absent for it is unjust.

Don't speak ill of someone who is not present to defend himself. It is unreasonable and not right.

The basis of good manners is God's love. Proverbs 17:9 says, "He that covereth a transgression seeketh love; but he that repeateth a matter separateth very friends." Speaking ill of anyone is not edifying to the listener. "Let no corrupt communication proceed out of your mouth, but that which is good to the use of edifying, that it may minister grace unto the hearers." (Ephesians 4:29) Two verses later we are commanded to not speak evil. "Let all bitterness, and wrath, and anger, and clamor, and evil speaking, be put away from you, with all malice." (Ephesians 4:31)

90. Being set at meat scratch not, neither spit, cough, or blow your nose except there's a necessity for it.

At a meal do not scratch yourself anywhere. Do not spit, cough, or blow your nose except when absolutely necessary.

91. Make no show of taking great delight in your victuals. Feed not with greediness. Cut your bread with a knife. Lean not on the table, neither find fault with what you eat.

Don't rave about the meal you are eating. Don't shovel the food into your mouth. Cut your bread with a knife (don't tear it). Don't lean on the table and don't complain about the food.

It is good to complement the cook (or cooks), but don't make a show of it. Don't act like this is the first meal you've had in weeks.

Shoveling food into your mouth shows the sin of gluttony. Giving in to appetite is a sin. Proverbs 23:1-2 shows us the gravity of this sin. "When thou sittest to eat with a ruler, consider diligently what is before thee: And put a knife to thy throat, if thou be a man given to appetite." In Deuteronomy 21, parents who had a rebellious adult child who would not listen to them were to bring him to the elders of the city for judgment. Stubbornness, rebellion, gluttony, and drunkenness are the sins listed. "And they shall say unto the elders of his city, This our son is stubborn and rebellious, he will not obey our voice; he is a glutton, and a drunkard. And all the men of his city shall stone him with stones, that he die: so shalt thou put evil away from among you; and all Israel shall hear, and fear." (Deuteronomy 21:20-21) They stoned him to death for those sins. We call gluttony "over eating" but God takes it a lot more seriously than just "eating a little too much."

Leaning on the table is not a rule mentioned in the Bible. Keeping elbows off the table seems to be acceptable in some circumstances today, such as when there is no food in front of you. While you are eating, you should not have your elbows on the table. When your elbows are off the table, you sit up straighter and don't get in your neighbor's way. You are less likely to bump anything accidentally and knock them into anyone's lap. It is all about considering others.

We should be thankful for what is put before us. Complaining shows a lack of gratefulness both to our hosts and to God. Philippians 2:14 tells us to do all things without complaining. First Corinthians 10:10 tells us not to murmur.

92. Take no salt or cut bread with your knife greasy.

Don't use a greasy knife to get salt or cut your bread. In Washington's day, they didn't use saltshakers. The salt was in a bowl shared by all. A greasy knife would leave grease in the salt bowl and cause it to clump together. The loaf of bread was also shared and didn't come in a plastic bag pre-sliced.

93. When entertaining anyone at table, it is decent to present him with meat. Undertake not to help others undesired by the master.

When hosting anyone (guest of honor) for a meal, it is good manners to serve him first. Don't help anyone else unless the host of the dinner says so.

94. If you soak bread in the sauce, let it be no more than what you put in your mouth at a time; and blow not your broth at table but stay till cools of itself.

If you soak or dip your bread in the sauce, let it be no more than one bite at a time. (This is probably where we get the idea of not dipping twice into a shared bowl.) Don't blow on broth or soup at the table. Let it cool by itself. If that prolongs the meal, so be it. It is better to stay longer at the table than to make a mess by blowing too hard on your food.

95. Put not your meat to your mouth with your knife in your hand neither spit forth the stones of any fruit pie upon a dish nor cast anything under the table.

Don't put food in your mouth while still holding your knife. Lay it down before taking the bite. Don't spit seeds of any fruit pie into a dish. Don't throw anything under the table.

These days we don't make fruit pies with the seeds still in the fruit, except maybe a berry pie with very small seeds. Throwing food under the table would make a mess for someone else to clean up. That would be extremely inconsiderate. Even if pets were there to eat it, it would be considered an insult to the cook or host to not eat what was on your plate.

96. It's unbecoming to stoop much to one's meat. Keep your fingers clean, and when foul, wipe them on a corner of your table napkin.

It is ill mannered to bend low over the table to eat. Keep your fingers clean. When you need to, wipe them on the corner of your napkin.

The rule I was told was "Fork to mouth, not mouth to fork." While it is good to lean in enough to keep from dropping your food in your lap, you should not lean so low that you seem to be eating from a trough.

Don't be messy when you eat. Your napkin is there for a reason; use it.

97. Put not another bit into your mouth till the former be swallowed. Let not your morsels be too big for the jowls.

Don't put another bite in your mouth until you have swallowed the previous one. Don't take bites too big for your jaws.

98. Drink not nor talk with your mouth full, neither gaze about you while you are a drinking.

Don't drink or talk with your mouth full. Swallow your food before you take a drink. Don't create a situation where chewed food might fall out of your mouth. Don't look around while drinking.

99. Drink not too leisurely nor yet too hastily. Before and after drinking wipe your lips. Breathe not then or ever with too great a noise, for its uncivil.

Don't drink too slowly nor too quickly. Before and after drinking, wipe your lips. Don't sigh then or ever with too loud a noise for it is uncivil.

To drink too slowly may mean holding the liquid in your mouth before swallowing. Drinking too quickly makes loud gulping sounds. Sighing loudly for any reason is inconsiderate of others. Purposely making loud sounds, whether gulping or sighing, is drawing attention to yourself. You are not to demand attention.

100. Cleanse not your teeth with the table cloth, napkin, fork, or knife but if others do it, let it be done with a pick tooth.

Don't clean your teeth with your napkin, fork, or knife. If others do it, let it be done with a toothpick.

Cleaning your teeth at the table with anything that is not intended for that purpose is inconsiderate of others. If you must clean your teeth, first leave the table. Use a toothpick, not anything else. If necessary, go brush your teeth.

101. Rinse not your mouth in the presence of others.

Don't swish your drink around in your mouth when in the presence of others.

102. It is out of use to call upon the company often to eat, nor need you drink to others every time you drink.

It is out of use to often tell the company to eat, nor do you need to toast others every time you drink.

103. In company of your betters be not longer in eating than they are. Lay not your arm, but only your hand upon the table.

In the company of your superiors don't take longer to eat than they do. Don't lay your arm (elbow) on the table, but only your hand.

104. It belongs to the chiefest in company to unfold his napkin and fall to meat first, but he ought then to begin in time and to dispatch with dexterity that the slowest may have time allowed him.

It is the responsibility of the host or hostess to unfold his napkin and begin eating first, but he/she ought to begin on time so that the slowest eater may have the necessary time allowed him.

105. Be not angry at table whatever happens and if you have reason to be so, show it not but on a cheerful countenance, especially if there be strangers, for good humor makes one dish of meat a feast.

Don't be angry at a meal whatever happens. If you have a reason to be angry, don't show it. Be cheerful, especially if there are strangers present, for a good attitude makes one dish of meat a feast.

106. Set not yourself at the upper of the table but if it be your due or that the master of the house will have it so, and contend not, lest you should trouble the company.

This is what Jesus said in Luke 14:8-11. "When thou art bidden of any man to a wedding, sit not down in the highest room; lest a more honorable man than thou be bidden of him; And he that bade thee and him come and say to thee, Give this man place; and thou begin with shame to take the lowest room. But when thou art bidden, go and sit down in the lowest room; that when he that bade thee cometh, he may say unto thee, Friend, go up higher: then shalt thou have worship in the presence of them that sit at meat with thee. For whosoever exalteth himself shall be abased; and he that humbleth himself shall be exalted. The second part of the manner is, "Don't argue about where you are seated and so bring animosity to the company."

107. If others talk at table, be attentive but talk not with meat in your mouth.

If others talk at a meal, pay attention. Don't talk with food in your mouth.

108. When you speak of God or His attributes, let it be seriously and with reverence. Honour and obey your natural parents although they be poor.

When you speak of God or His attributes, be serious and reverent. Honor and obey your parents regardless of their social status.

The Bible tells us to fear God. The Hebrew word is yârê' (yaw-ray'). It means both to fear and to revere. In

Leviticus 19:14 we are commanded to show our fear and reverence for God by not cursing the deaf or putting a stumbling block before the blind. Again in 19:32 we are to show it by rising and honoring the gray haired and the old man. Leviticus 25:17 says we are to show it by not oppressing each other. This word for oppress means "to rage or be violent; by implication to suppress to maltreat." *Jamieson, Fausset, Brown Commentary* says, "This related to the sale or purchase of possessions and the duty of paying an honest and equitable regard, on both sides, to the limited period during which the bargain could stand. The object of the legislator was, as far as possible, to maintain the original order of families, and an equality of condition among the people." Being honest in business dealings and not taking advantage of others shows a reverence for God. Leviticus 25:36 says that lending without interest shows a reverence for God. Leviticus 25:43 tells people in authority to show their reverence by not ruling with severity.

Speaking of God seriously means we don't make jokes about God or His character. If Jesus were standing beside you in person, would you speak of Him in such a way? He is there with you. He hears everything you say. He knows it before it ever comes out of your mouth. He will hold you accountable for your words.

Speaking of God reverently means with humility and in submission to His authority as your Creator and Judge. Remember we are His ambassadors, His witnesses (2 Corinthians 5:20). We do not want to misrepresent Him by showing a lack of reverence for Him.

109. Let your recreations be manful, not sinful.

Let your recreation and entertainment be mannerly and courageous, not sinful. That is, do not let your entertainment have anything to do with behaviors the Bible has called sin.

Psalm 101 is a perfect guide for entertainment as well as our choice of friends.

> I will sing of mercy and judgment: unto Thee, O LORD, will I sing. I will behave myself wisely in a perfect way. O when wilt Thou come unto me? I will walk within my house with a perfect heart. I will set no wicked thing before mine eyes: I hate the work of them that turn aside; it shall not cleave to me. A froward heart shall depart from me: I will not know a wicked person. Whoso privily slandereth his neighbor, him will I cut off: him that hath an high look and a proud heart will not I suffer. Mine eyes shall be upon the faithful of the land, that they may dwell with me: he that walketh in a perfect way, he shall serve me. He that worketh deceit shall not dwell within my house: he that telleth lies shall not tarry in my sight. I will early destroy all the wicked of the land; that I may cut off all wicked doers from the city of the LORD. (Psalms 101:1-8)

Two verses that I was taught to apply to my reading, music, movies, television, etc. are these. "Whether therefore ye eat, or drink, or whatsoever ye do, do all to the glory of God." (1 Corinthians 10:31) "And whatsoever ye do in word or deed, do all in the name of the Lord Jesus, giving thanks to God and the Father by Him." (Colossians 3:17) Apply these Scriptures to all your entertainment and it will be easy to avoid sin.

110. Labor to keep alive in your breast that little spark of celestial fire called conscience.

Work to keep your conscience alive and alert.

Here are some Bible verses about conscience.

(Paul before Felix at Caesarea) "And herein do I exercise myself, to have always a conscience void of offence toward God, and toward men." (Acts 24:16)

"This charge I commit unto thee, son Timothy, according to the prophecies which went before on thee, that thou by them mightest war a good warfare; Holding faith, and a good conscience; which some having put away concerning faith have made shipwreck." (1 Timothy 1:18-19)

"Likewise must the deacons be grave, not double-tongued, not given to much wine, not greedy of filthy lucre; Holding the mystery of the faith in a pure conscience." (1 Timothy 3:8-9)

"Now the Spirit speaketh expressly, that in the latter times some shall depart from the faith, giving heed to seducing spirits, and doctrines of devils; Speaking lies in hypocrisy; having their conscience seared with a hot iron; Forbidding to marry, and commanding to abstain from meats, which God hath created to be received with thanksgiving of them which believe and know the truth." (First Timothy 4:1-3)

"I thank God, whom I serve from my forefathers with pure conscience, that without ceasing I have remembrance of thee in my prayers night and day." (Second Timothy 1:3)

"Unto the pure all things are pure: but unto them that are defiled and unbelieving is nothing pure; but even their mind and conscience is defiled. They profess that they know God; but in works they deny him, being abominable, and disobedient, and unto every good work reprobate." (Titus 1:15-16)

From these verses we learn that it does indeed take diligent labor to keep a living, active conscience. Our consciences can be turned off or seared. They can be defiled so that they don't identify sin as sin. To keep our consciences alive we must stay in the Word. By that I mean to daily, actively read and study the Bible. We must also listen to our consciences. When a person continually refuses to obey his or her conscience, its voice is silenced. This is described in Romans 1:28, "And even as they did not like to retain God in their knowledge, God gave them over to a reprobate mind, to do those things which are not convenient." A reprobate mind is one that has ungodly, worthless thinking. It is defined as "very wicked or lewd." We do not want a reprobate mind that rejects God and good manners.

It is the voice of our conscience that makes us use good manners and treat others with decency and respect. We must keep it alive.

The Rules of Civility

by Antoine de Courtin

Also called The Rules of Civility or, Certain Ways of
Deportment observed in France, amongst all Persons of
Quality, upon several Occasions

Translated out of French.

The Third Edition with Additions.

LONDON,

Printed for J. Martyn at the Bell in St. Paul's
Churchyard, and John Starkey at the Mitre in Fleet
Street, near Temple Bar.

MDCLXXV

(1675)

THE ADVERTISEMENT

This treatise was never intended for the press, but in answer to a gentleman of Provence, who being the author's particular friend, desired some few precepts of civility for his son, at that time come newly from the Academy, and designed for the Court.

The publication was judged useful, not only to such as had children to bring up, but to others also, who though advanced in years, might be defective notwithstanding, in the exactness and punctilio of civility, so indispensably necessary in the conversation of the world.

Upon which consideration he was induced to super add something to the ladies also, that both sexes might participate of the profit. But as this work cannot have relation to any but the gentry, even so to them it is presented in a different manner: For, there being many persons (he is sensible) to whom these rules are unnecessary, and who, if they pleased, could exhibit much better directions; to them it is he does most earnestly apply himself, that they would not only correct what is corrigible in his, but transmit to the printer what other notes and observations, upon this subject, they shall make of their own; to the end that if it be judged worthy of a second impression, it may come forth more copious and complete.

For other, who not having opportunity or convenience of repairing to Court, and learning these rudiments of civility in their proper school; our hope is with the least docibility (without which they are capable of nothing) they will reap their advantage, and thank us for our design of gratifying them.

And that the success of this enterprise might correspond the better to the design, it is not impertinent to advertise, that whilst this treatise was in the press, there was another put forth, entitled *The Education of a Prince*; which was the labors of two of the most eminent wits of our age. It would not be amiss, I say, if this treatise were perused, to impregnate our minds, and dispose them to the practice of such virtues as are necessary for our several conditions; that so our civility being laid upon a solid foundation, may be a real ornament to our prudence and learning; whereas without the concomitancy of virtue, is nothing else but a phantasm, or masquerade.

But above all, it would be convenient, if we not only peruse, but study, and that accurately, *The Treatise of Christian Civility*, very properly bound up with the two other, and not so short and succinct; which two books, by the seasonableness of their edition, seemed to be put out by these excellent masters, in assistance to mind: For theirs comprehending the theory and general principles of civility, and mine the particular practice; theirs serving as the first part, and mine as the second; betwixt both, the work may be complete, if it be no arrogance to add a piece, low in its price, and inconsiderable in its material, to a fabric of intrinsical riches, and of incomparable architecture.

The Rules of Civility:

OR

Certain Ways of Deportment observed in France among all Persons of Quality, upon several Occasions.

To a Gentleman of Provence.

It is your desire, Sir, to know of me what is that polite and ingenuous behavior, which is so laudably requisite in a well-bred man; because, say you, I am well versed in the manners of the world, and acquainted (according to your observation) with the rules of civility and respect. I will not defend myself against your good opinion; yet I cannot but fear my compliance will convince you, it was your friendship (not any merit of mine) which prepossessed you in my favor.

Chapter 1
What is Civility?

In obedience therefore to your commands, let me tell you, the gentleness and plausibility, of which you desire information, is in my opinion nothing else, but the modesty and decorum to be observed by everyone according to his condition: for your curiosity is not (I conceive) about the *bonne Grace*, or the neat and becoming air; which is as it were natural to some persons, who by a particular bounty of nature, have a way of pleasing in whatever they do, and displeasing nobody. Precepts for the acquisition of this air, and agreeableness, are not to be given, it being a peculiar gift (expressed in this sentence: *Gaudeant benenati*) which nature reserves to herself, and is almost the only thing which art cannot imitate.

But the pleasing of the corporal eye being but a trifle, unless we can order things so as to make ourselves grateful to the eye of the soul; it is not that outward address or becomingness which is the true principle and form of a gentleman; it is something more substantial and solid, which discovers the disposition of our soul, rather than the gesticulations of our body. In short, should we look no further than this exterior grace, it would follow, that those who have any corporal incommodity, would pass for monsters among men; whereas their souls being well cultivated and polite, their actions may be as pleasing as the actions of the handsomest man.

1. Neque enim folum corporis qui ad naturam apti funt, fed multò etiam magis animi motus probandi, qui item ad naturam apcommodati funt .*Cic. lib.* 1. *Off.*

To establish therefore the rules of true generosity, I find we have no more to do, but to apply to the rules of civility; which civility being nothing but a certain modesty and *pudor* required in all our actions; it is of that virtue properly we are to give description; and that a description would be sufficient to direct towards the acquisition of that politeness, that agreeableness, that I know not what, which has power to conciliate the applause and affections of all people in spite of any natural or accidental deformity.

1. Modefita eft per quam pudor honefta-tis claram & ftabilem comparat auctoritatem. *Cic. Rb.*

77

Chapter 2
The Definition, Circumstances, and Different Kinds of Civility.

Civility is defined, *A Science in instructing how to dispose all our words and actions in their proper and true places*. But nothing can be said or done exactly, and with Civility, without four circumstances be observed. First, *that everyone behave himself according to his age and condition*. Secondly, *That respect be preserved to the quality of the person with whom we converse*. Thirdly, *That we consider the time; and* fourthly, *the place where we are*. These circumstances relating to the knowledge of ourselves and other people, and to the observation of times and places, are of such necessary importance, that if any of the four be deficient, all our actions (how well intended soever) are but deformed and imperfect.

1. Scientia earum rerum quæ agentur aut dicentur, loco fuo collocandarum. *Cic. Lib. 1. Off.*

But it would be no easy matter to prescribe rules of civility so exact, as that they should comply with all times, persons, and places in the world; seeing nothing is more obvious than variety of customs, and that what is decent in one nation, is indecent in another; what is useful, and perhaps profitable in one age, declines, and grows contemptible in the next; in short, nothing is so intrinsically decorous, but the experience or capriccio of mankind alters, or explodes it.

By reason of this variety, our resolution is to treat of it as it stands at this time in reputation among Christians; after which, by some few distinctions we shall elaborate and prepare it for practice.

As to the manner of deportment at coronations, entries, cavalcades, and all public ceremonies, we refer to the heralds, public officers, or such as in their travels have made them their particular observation. The conducting of Ambassadors, the formalities at installments, creation of magistrates, and such kind of solemnities, being no part of my present province; your command, nor my design reaching no farther than some short directions for particular demeanor.

To come then to the point, and explain ourselves in as few words as we may: This modesty or civility we speak of, if taken right, is nothing else but humility; which being well practiced by persons of honor, (for there is no quality, no estate, no pedigree [that] exempts any man from the exercise of virtue: and indeed the greatest persons are but mean and despicable amongst wise men, if they be not ennobled thereby) this virtue, is sufficient to pronounce a man civil, and a gentleman.

This humility consists not only in a moderate and submiss opinion of ourselves, but in preferring the satisfaction and commodity of other people before our own, and that so ingeniously; that we cannot provoke or disoblige anyone without great trouble and horror; and to be of this disposition, is to be truly modest; the reason is, because as there is nothing lessens, or makes a man more insupportable, that insolence and vanity; so there is nothing recommends him so strongly to the affections of all people, as affability and submission. It is a character God Almighty has imprinted in all the virtues which spring from Him, to affect the eyes, and allure the heart of all such as are beholders of their practice; and amongst all these virtues, this of humility has that privilege in extraordinary eminence; from whence it happens, though a person of known modesty and humility be guilty of any formal indecency in his carriage, it shall be so far from being objected to his disparagement, that everyone will endeavor to excuse it: whereas on the other side, a proud and imperious person, adorned with never so much breeding, and beautified with never so much art, displeases all people, and is unwelcome wherever he goes.

     1 Modeſtia provenit ex quadam dulcedine affectus, qua quis horret omne quod poteſt alium contriſtare. *S. Th.* 2. 2. quæſt. 157. *Art.* 3.
     Juſtitiæ partes ſunt non violare hominem, verecundiæ non offendere. *Cic. lib.* 1. *Off.*

Modesty therefore is the effect of humility, as civility and the gratefulness of our actions is the effect of our modesty.

Chapter 3
The Difference Between Decent and Indecent Things According to Custom.

To this must be added, the difference between things civil and uncivil, convenient and inconvenient; for let a man be never so humble, if he be stupid at the same time, or morose, he shall never pass for either civil or modest, nor be ever admitted into the conversation of gentlemen.

For the better distinction between decent and indecent things, it is principally to be desired, our gentleman should have a good natural judgment and perception to discern the various qualities of things; for (because) for want of that many times we mistake and fall into absurdities, taking things for mysteries and miracles of wit, which among sober and judicious people, are but trivial and vain.

In the next place it is necessary an exact observation be taken of what is owned and established for civil or uncivil, in the place where we are.

In the third place, regard is to be had not to confound familiarity and civility.

For the first there are no precepts to be given, it being a natural gift without the assistance of art; only it is rectified and improved by education sometimes, and extraordinary inspection upon ourselves.

The second, if formed both of the general consent and practice of all well-bred men, and certain peculiar rules of decency which nature has likewise inscribed. Her also we are to follow as our model and guide, observing her prescripts in things which are honorable, and her modesty and retention in things which are otherwise.

> 1 Quod fi fequamur ducem naturam, nunquam aberrabimus. *Cic. ib.*

For example, so strong an obligation has she laid upon us to conduct ourselves according to her directions, that if we deviate and transgress her rules,

> 2 Admodum autem tuenda funt fua cuique non vitiofa, fed tamen propria, quo facilius decorum tueatur. *Ib.*

either in word or action, (as it happens to such as counterfeit the greatness or smallness of their voice, as they think it more commendable, or affect any particular postures or motions in their marches or other gesture) that constraint and irregularity immediately displeases, and by common consent, and a natural inclination in all people to integrity and truth, is found immediately indecent.

1 Id. maxime quemquem decet, quod eſt
cujuſque ſuum maxime *Cic. ib.* In omni
genere quæ ſunt recta & ſimplicia laudantur.
Ib. C.

Furthermore, nature having a desire to conceal some
parts of our bodies, and to prevent some kind of
actions; custom and use are so well agreed to concur,
that the person who should publicly discover them,
would appear the most ungenteel man in the world;
so strong a caution has she laid upon us of acting or
speaking nothing contrary to her dictates of honor
and modesty.

2 Quæ enim natura occultavit, eadem
omnes, qui ſana mente ſunt, removent ab o-
culis, ipſique neceſſitati dant operam, ut
quam occultiſſime pareant. *Cic. Ib.*

For other actions where nature has not been so
precise, but left us the same liberty with other
creatures, as in spitting, coughing, sneezing, eating,
drinking, etc. we may follow our own fancies,
because every man is naturally convinced the more
remote and contrary his actions are to the example of
brutes, the nearer does he approach to that perfection
to which man tends by natural propensity, according
to the preeminence of his nature.

For as there are some actions naturally indispensable,
and must be done, how indecent soever they be in
themselves, it is required they be performed with as
much modesty and remoteness from the practice of
beasts as possible.

84

Other things there are which have no dependency of nature, but have been introduced and allowed in all times among us, as to pull off one's hat in testimony of respect; to give superiors or equals the precedence; to allow them the upper end of the table or chamber, and the wall as they walk in the streets. These are things so generally expected, and so essential to civility, that if a man does not resolute a person which hath saluted him with his hat, though his condition be ever so mean, he will be looked upon as uncivil and ill bred, let his extraction be never so great.

The third thing we have thought necessary, consists in a judicious discrimination of familiarity and respect; and this distinction is of the more importance, because upon some occasions familiarity may be decent and becoming, and at others presumptuous and troublesome.

Wherefore it is not inconvenient first to understand, that *familiarity is a genteel liberty between persons acting or discoursing together, by which it is tacitly and reciprocally agreed to take that in good part, which in strictness at other times, or in other company, might possibly displease.*

It is moreover to be observed that all humane conversation passes between equals, or superior and inferior; and that all transaction whatever is managed between persons of long, little, or no acquaintance at all.

Between equals, if one knows how to manage it well, familiarity is laudable; if but a little, it is dangerous; if not at all, it is rude, and discovers weakness of judgment.

From an inferior to a superior (unless he knows him extremely well, or if but a little, by his express command) familiarity is sauciness; and if he knows him not at all, impudence in the highest.

From superior to inferior, familiarity is graceful, and obliges the person which receives it.

So then, according to these remarks, all our actions in respect of other persons are either absolute and independent, or dependent according to the difference of superiority, equality, or inferiority. To the first, all things are lawful because they command to the others; and having no right to censure, the inferior must be contented to suffer. The second are at liberty among themselves; but the third are more particularly obliged to the rules of modesty.

For these reasons the two first may be familiar without indecorum, but the third never, without express order from the person on whom he depends.

But as these general principles would be of good service to such persons as knew how to apply them in all their conversations, so likewise it must be proportionably useful, if I reduce them to some heads, and make them more plain and intelligible thereby.

Here therefore we will commence our essay, in proposing an example of the converse between an inferior and superior, with whom there is no intimate acquaintance; this being the case which requires and affords more precepts than either of the other. Let us begin then with a young gentleman, whom we are to polish for the visiting and conversing with great persons, in all places, and at all times shall occur.

Chapter 4
Entrance Into a Great Person's House; Observations at the Door, in the Anti-chambers, and Elsewhere

To begin with the door of a prince, or great person, it is uncivil to knock hard or to give more than one knock.

At the door of his bedchamber or closet, to knock is no less than brutish; the way is to scratch only with their nails.

When he scratches with his nails at the king's bedchamber door, or any other great person's, and the usher demands his name, he must tell him his surname only, without the qualification of Mr. S. or my lord.

When he comes into a great man's house or chamber, it is not civil to wrap himself up in his cloak; but in the king's court he runs great hazard of correction.

It is boldness to enter of himself without being introduced.

If it be of importance to him to enter, and there be nobody to introduce him, he must try gently whether the door be locked or bolted on the inside; if it be, he is not to knock, or fiddle about the lock, like an impatient person, as if he would pick it, but he must patiently expect till it be opened, or scratch softly to make them hear; if nobody come, he must retire to some distance, lest being found about the door, he should be taken as an eavesdropper or spy, which would be great offence to all persons of quality.

It is but civil to walk with his hat off in the halls and antechambers, and this is to be observed, he who enters is obliged always to salute the first.

It is contrary to civility to bid a person [his superior] to put on his hat; and on the other side, the incivility is no less if in putting on his own hat, he makes not the person to whom he is speaking put on his also, though he be his inferior, if he be not his dependent.

When the king or queen's tables are spread, it is corrigible to keep on his hat, as likewise when the officers come by with the covering or meat.

It is rude to drink to a lady of your own, much more of greater quality, than yourself, with your hat on; and to be covered when she is drinking to you. When dinner is going up to any nobleman's table where you are a stranger, or of inferior quality, it is civil and good manners to be uncovered.

When anyone of extraordinary quality is present, it is uncivil to whisper, or to turn your face as if you were going to do it.

To laugh, talk, or ask questions at music entertainments is disobliging and unkind; for they are showing all their excellencies for your diversion, and striving which shall excel in that, which you are to judge; besides the noise and disturbance you make is offensive to them that are more attentive.

It is to affront a man, when he is in the middle of a serious discourse, to fall in talk to some in company of another matter.

In any room where our superiors are, it is not good manners to sit down unless desired [asked to].

In the bedchamber, he must be always uncovered: In the queen's chamber, the ladies which enter make their reverences towards the bed, to which it is not permitted any of them to approach, though there be no rails or balusters about it.

As to the ladies, it is convenient for them to know that besides the punctilio of their courtesies, there is the ceremony of the mask, the hoods, and the trains; for it is no less than rudeness in a woman to enter into anyone's chamber, to whom she owes any respect, with her gown tucked up, with her mask upon her face, or a hood about her head, unless it be thin and perspicuous.

It is to be strictly observed likewise, that their courtesies be not short and precipitate; but grave and low, if there be room, if it be only in passing, a moderate inclination is sufficient.

It is not civil to have their masks on before persons of honor in any place where they may be seen, unless they be in the same coach together at the same time.

It is uncivil to keep their masks on when they are saluting anyone, unless it be at a good distance: But even in that case they pull it off before any person of the blood [royalty].

In the chamber of any great person where the bed is railed in, it is rudeness to sit down upon the rails.

It is indiscretion also to lean upon the arms of the king's chair, or to loll upon the back of it; to prevent which, it is commonly turned towards the wall.

While he attends in the antechamber, or presence chamber, it is not decent to walk up and down in the room, and if at any time he does so, it is the usher's duty, and common practice to rebuke him.

It is no less absurd to whistle or sing for his divertissement [entertainment] (as they call it) while he is waiting in those rooms, or in the street, or any other place where there is concourse of people.

Chapter 5
Regulations for
Company Conversation

As it is a token of indiscretion and vanity for one to enter boldly and without ceremony into a room where people are in discourse (though he be of their acquaintance) unless his business be extraordinary, and he can steal in without disturbing them. It is the mark of incogitance or ill breeding when one comes into a room, to ball out as their throats would spit, to the person of their acquaintance: "your servant Sir; your humble servant, Madam; I wish you good day." But he must enter quietly and civilly, and when he comes near the person he would salute, make his complement modestly and gravely, without any such noise or obstreperousness.

If they do him the civility to rise when he comes in, he must have extraordinary care [that] he takes not any of their places, but seats himself upon another, and rather behind than before anybody; observing still not to sit down till they be all in their places; it being great indecorum to sit down in that case, while any person which gave him that respect continues upon his legs.

Less tolerable it is to enquire what they were talking of; or (if they be in discourse) to interrupt them, and enquire hastily, "What's that? Who did? Who said so?" especially if they be whispering or talking in private.

It is rash, and favors of a hair-brained humor, for anyone to ask another in the middle of a story, what was the beginning.

At first coming into a room, it is very unmannerly to salute any women in the company except your own acquaintance, for there may be some of too great quality for your approach, who you may ignorantly offend.

In visiting a lady lately come out of the country, or after a journey, it is not enough to salute her, but her gentlewoman also, if she be then present. But this ought especially to be observed among the sex.

If one be in company, it is not civil to speak to anyone of them, (or to any servant that comes in by accident) in a language the rest do not understand.

It is not civil to whisper in company, and less to laugh when you have done; for people being generally conscious, are apt to apply it to themselves, and conceive sometimes so great displeasure as is not easily removed.

I think it scarce necessary to set down the documents which are given every day to children; as whenever they answer yes or no, to give always the titles of Sir, Madam, or My Lord, as they are due; as yes Sir, no Madam, etc. It is handsome also when one is to contradict any person of quality, and to answer in the negative it is not to be done bluntly with a "No, Sir, that is not so," but by circumlocution, as "Pardon me Sir, I beg your pardon Madam, if I presume to say, fisking and prattling are but ill ways to please."

It is obvious too, that it is but a rustic and clownish kind of wit to put Sir, or Madam after any word so as to render his meaning ambiguous, as to say, "this book is bound in calf, Sir; this is a fine mare, Madam; or he is mounted upon an ass, My Lord," etc.

It is not handsome to add after the titles of Sir, or Madam, the surname, or quality of the person one speaks to, as to say, "Yes, Mr. Cicero; No Mr. Consul," but rather, "yes Sir, no Sir," and no more.

When one speaks anything complementally, or runs out into extravagant expression in commendation of the person to whom he speaks, it is not civil to say, "you jeer me, Sir," but the phrase must be altered, and one may say, "you amaze me, Sir," etc.

When one tells any story or action of another, especially if it be to the disadvantage of the person who did it, it is not good to father it upon [tell it to] the person to whom we are speaking, expressly, or under his own name; but to do it more remotely, and by some indefinite term, as to say, "Such a thing was done rashly, such a thing had been more obligingly let alone;" is better than to tell him bluntly, "he was mad to do such a thing, or he disobliged such a man in doing so and so."

Great care is to be had likewise of speaking imperiously, or using any words of command towards the person to whom we are speaking; we are rather to accustom ourselves to a way of circumlocution, by varying the phrase in some other indefinite manner; as instead of saying, "Come, go, do, or say such a thing," we must say, "if you think it convenient, come; you will do well to go; in my judgment it would be well to do so."

It is no small argument of indiscretion, in a person that should be thought otherwise, to magnify, or talk much of his wife, his children or relations in the company of persons of quality; nor before any company, especially of strangers; yet perhaps you may hear some say to this effect; "Good lack, how did I laugh last night at my Robbin; I did not think it possible for a child to have so much wit; I believe he hath too much wit to live," etc. This betrays an ignorance in a man's behavior, and such like discourse seldom pleases any but themselves, though they may be spoken of upon occasion, if it be done pertinently, and without extravagant commendation.

It is not handsome to appear affected, or overmuch pleased with the commendations of ones relations; nor when one speaks of his own wife, to mention her by her name or quality, or any term of familiarity used between themselves; as for example, it would not be handsome if Cicero, or any president were speaking of his wife, for him to say, "Madam Cicero did so; Madam la Presidente said this; or, my joy, my duck went hither or thither;" but much better it would be to say only "my wife." A wife speaking of her husband before persons of ordinary condition, may call him by his name, with the addition of Master, if he uses that title; but before persons of quality, she is to say only "my husband." The man which caresses, or expresses much fondness, to his wife before company makes himself ridiculous.

It is not civil to enquire too particularly of the husband after his wife unless she has been absent in the country, or desperately ill; especially if he is a person for whom we ought to have any respect.

If it happens we are bound in civility to inquire of the husband, we must proceed contrary to his way; for whereas he in discretion is to say no more than "my wife" in speaking of her, we must not follow his example and cry rudely, "how old is your wife?" or "how does your wife?" but observing the quality of the husband, say "how old is my lady your wife? I wish My Lady President or My Lady Duchess much happiness."

Nor is it good manners to ask any person, especially a woman, how old she is; for all that are old would be thought otherwise, at least not to undergo the infirmities thereof.

Avoid unsuitable and hyperbolical commendations of any person. For any excess nauseates, and it will be a kind of detraction from those you speak to and bears with it a tincture of arrogance. For he that commends another would have him esteemed upon his judgment: it is necessary for him that doth it to reflect upon his own repute; for it disparages a wise man to be commended by a fool, not is it any credit for a good man to be commended by a debauchee.

Being in the company of persons of quality, unless one be of greater dignity himself, it is not less ridiculous to mention one's relations, with their titles of honor (though we ought always to speak of them with respect) as to say, "My Lord My father," or "My Lady My mother." They are only to be called "my father, my mother;" nor is it proper for children of any bigness to call them Dad or Mom; much less to call them by their names or their titles.

When one speaks to a third person of any person of quality who is present, it is not civil to name him bluntly if he stands by; as for example, if I were speaking to Cicero of Caesar, in the presence of Caesar, and should tell him, "Caesar had done great things in France;" and Cicero should ask me, "who took Gergovia?" I must not nod my head and cry "He;" that would be a disobligation to Caesar, and favor too much of contempt: But I must answer, this gentleman took it; and it is no less uncivil to point with one's finger to the person of whom we are speaking, if he be in the room.

It is improper likewise to send commendations or messages to anybody by our superiors; but we must rather find out some other person that is either equal or inferior.

It is defect of civility likewise, and good breeding, to interrupt any person that is our superior, if he be in discourse; and makes us ridiculous to speak in that case, but when we are spoken to.

When a person of superior quality asks a question in company where there are many more our superiors, it is arrogance to answer first, though the question be but trivial as "what is it a clock? [what time is it?] what day is it?" Even in those questions we are to give precedence to our betters, unless they be made particularly to us.

If a person for whom we bear any common respect hesitates in his discourse to consider what he has to say, or to rub up his memory; it is rude to cut him off quite, or interrupt him, though in his assistance; as if one were telling that "Caesar defeated Pompey in the Battle of, of, of," it would be unhandsome for one to clap in and cry "Pharsalus;" he ought rather to attend till he be asked.

In the same manner, it is not genteel to rectify a superior though he be in a mistake, because it would look like a kind of contradiction; as if he should say, "It was a testimony of good nature in Darius, to weep when he saw Alexander dead." Where Darius is mistaken for Alexander, we are obliged in civility to attend till he recollects himself or gives us occasion to undeceive him; and then we are to do it without any reflection.

In speaking to a person, it is not civil to cry, "You understand me, I hope? Do you understand me? I do not know whether I explain myself sufficiently." One must say nothing in that nature but proceed in his discourse; and if he perceive he does not understand, repeat, or illustrate what he said before in as few words as possible.

In relating any story, it is ridiculous to say almost at every word, he said, or she said.

Caution must be had likewise of speaking anything [that] may perplex or trouble anyone; or remembering or reviving any affair, that is not to the advantage of the person to whom they speak.

To sleep, go away, or gape, while one is speaking, is not only uncivil but stupid; and to be laughing and playing the fool is as bad. Care, therefore, must be had not to play with ones fingers, to play or toy with him that sits next [to you], nor do any childish thing to provoke him to laugh; lest the company being indisposed for such idle diversions, take pet [offense] and be gone.

If a person of quality be in the company of ladies, it is too juvenile and light to play with them, to toss or tumble them; to kiss them by surprise, to force away their hoods, their fans, or their muffs.

It is unhandsome among ladies, or any other serious company, to throw off one's cloak, to pull off one's perruque [wig], or doublet, to cut one's nails, to tie one's garter, to change shoes, if they pinch; to call for one's nightgown and slippers to be at ease, nor sing between the teeth [whistle?], nor drum with one's fingers; all which are as incongruous, as for an officer of horse to appear in shoes when he is called to attend the general.

It is unpleasing, likewise, to hear a man always complaining of his distempers in company; and implies either stupidity or hypocrisy; it being to be supposed, he does it either by that vain and impertinent pretense, to conceal his want of ability to maintain any discourse; or that he may be thereby permitted to take his own ease though to the disturbance of the rest of the company.

When any jewel or other rarity is shown to the company, it is indecent to clap one's hand upon it to see it first; it being much better manners to moderate our curiosity, and expect patiently till it comes to our turn, and when it does, it argues no great discretion to admire it too much, or to run out into any extravagant commendations, as some people do, who by their immoderate transport, convince us they have seen nothing curious before, and have no true estimate of the value of things.

On the other side, to be cold and indifferent in praising what is really commendable, is a sign of sullenness and morosity, especially in great persons, and is ungrateful to all the world; the best way therefore, is to be modest and just, and to give things their approbation as they think them to deserve it.

It is not improper to advertise in this place, that when anything is presented to one by a superior or equal, it is decent to receive it with his glove off, kissing his hand; as also when he returns it, or presents anything to another: but if a thing be desired of us, the best way is to deliver it immediately, without making him expect.

When a curiosity is once produced among company, it is uncivil to put it up till all have seen it that are desirous.

It is barbarous, and argues the height of indiscretion, to peep over one's shoulder when he is writing, and ungenteel when he is reading, and fond to cast his eyes seriously upon any papers lying in his way.

It is not handsome, likewise, to come too near those who are telling of money; any trunk that is open, or any closet where jewels or such rarities are laid.

1 *Ni los ojos à las cartas; ni las manos à las arcas refranes.*

In like manner, if one be in his closet with any person who is suddenly called out, it is civil to go out with him, and attend his return in some other room.

It is incivility before a person of quality to read any letter or other paper that is brought to him, unless the said person be concerned therein, or does expressly desire it.

If new company comes in, or any person rises to be gone, or to pay respect to them that are entering, though they be our inferiors, it is but civility to rise also.

If anyone comes in to speak with us from a person for whom we ought to have respect, though it be but a footman, we are obliged in civility to rise from our seat and receive his message with our hats off.

If we be obliged to go and come into the room before persons of quality, we are to have a care of turning our backs upon them, and are to endeavor to go out backwards as much as we can.

Late custom has dispensed with a rule of civility, which is solemn taking of leave at departure from company. When many are met together at a visit, and some are discoursing, or others at cards, it is not unmannerly to rise and only take leave of the lady you gave the visit to, and go without speaking to any of the rest, except they rise up.

It is of late, likewise, observed not to call any gentlewoman by her surname, adding only madam to it, but rather Mrs. as not "Madam Joan, what's a clock? [what time is it?]" but "what is't a clock

[What time is it,] Madam?" Not my service to Madam Smith, but rather to Mrs. Smith.

But above all things, our principal care must be of intruding upon persons in private discourse, which will be discovered either by their retirement, their whispering, or by the changing their discourse upon our approach; having observed either of these signs, we are presently to withdraw upon penalty of falling into great indiscretion.

For companies met upon any solemnity or ceremony, we must take specially notice of two sorts of people; the authors of the ceremony, or the persons invited.

To the authors in the first place, if the ceremony be any serious matter, we must always give place, though they be our inferiors. For example, at a wedding the bride, bridegroom, their relations, and the ecclesiastical persons have always the preeminence; and we are in civility obliged to do them though they be very much beneath us. If it be at a christening, the god-fathers, god-mothers, child, widwife [midwife], and such of the matrons as are most essential to the ceremony, are in equity to precede. If it be a funeral, the relations of the dead persons are in course to go first and have the most honorable place; if it be at an offering, or religious procession, the church wardens and other officers of the church are to be in the van [front].

As to the persons invited, if we be of that number, we are not to place ourselves, if there be anybody else to dispose of us; but if there be none, but everybody is left at his own liberty, it is discretion to leave the best places void for persons of greater quality; unless we be of such a dignity and character as obliges us, according to custom to stand upon our punctilios, not so much out of an opinion of ourselves, as in consideration of the honor we owe to the society, of which we are members, or to the prince whose minsters we are.

In short, in regard of all sorts of people, our civility concerning the place ought to be regulated upon a right estimation, first of ourselves, and then of other persons. It is commonly looked upon as civility to give place, or at least offer it, to ecclesiastical persons in reference to their functions; to such magistrates as are in their prince's name entrusted with the execution of his laws; to persons of any public character; to persons of extraordinary extraction; to women; to ancient persons; and such as have rendered themselves egregious by any faculty of their own.

Chapter 6
Conduct Towards a Great Person

As to our behavior towards great persons of more than ordinary quality, it is to be observed when we enter into their chambers or closets, we must go in gently, making a profound reverence and inclination of our bodies, if the person be present; if not, we are not to peep and pry up and down to see what we can discover; but to retire as softly as we came in, and expect his appearance without.

ɪ Incivile eſt illum falutare qúi reddit uɾinam, aut alvum exonerat. *Eraſ.Coll. in Princ.*

If the person we visit be sick, and in bed, we must return, without we be desired to enter; and then having seem him, our visit is to be short, because sick people are unquiet, and tied up to their physic and times: we must remember likewise to speak low, and provoke him to answer as little as we can.

We must remember it is great indecency to sit down upon the bed, especially if it be a woman's; but above all, it has been unhandsome in all ages, and favors of want of breeding, if being in company of our superiors, equals, or other persons with whom we have not a perfect familiarity, we throw ourselves upon the bed, and continue our discourse as we are lolling there.

If the person upon whom we wait be writing, reading, or studying, it is not manners to interrupt him presently with our discourse; but we must rather stay till he has done, or leaves off of himself to entertain us.

If we be desired to sit, we must do it, but with some little demonstration of unwillingness, in regard of our respect; and be sure to place ourselves beneath him towards the lower end of the room, which is always next to the door where we came in; and the upper end is where the person of honor sits himself.

It must not be forgotten also that when we do sit, it be upon a seat inferior to his, if it be to be had; there being great difference to be observed between a chair with arms, a back chair, and a joint-stool; the first being most honorable, the second the next, and the stool the lowest of the three.

It is altogether unhandsome to appear, especially before women, without our waistcoat and shirt so open as that our skin may be seen; or to come in with any other part gaping, that ought in modesty to be shut.

When one sits down, he is not to place himself cheek by jowl by his side, but just over against him, that he may take notice of his readiness to hear him; and because it is not so handsome to sit full in his face, it will be esteemed good breeding, if he place himself *en profite* or something sideways.

You must have a care to avoid in ordering your speech and whispers, so that none of your breath may come near his nose when you speak, lest you offend him.

We must by no means put on our hats, unless commanded; we must have our gloves upon our hands, and keep ourselves quiet upon our seats, without playing with our legs, our band strings, our hat, or our gloves; not picking or poltering in our nose, nor scratching of any other part.

We must have a care of yawning, of blowing our nose, or spitting, especially if the room be rubbed; and if it falls out so, as we cannot avoid it, we must do it in our handkerchief, turning aside, and holding our hat or left hand before our face, and be sure not to look upon it when we have done.

[I am not sure what a room being rubbed means. The only definition of "rub" I found in the dictionaries was "to wipe hard." I assume a rubbed room was one that had been thoroughly cleaned.]

We are not to take snuff before any person of honor (who has privilege to take it before us) unless he presents it himself; in that case it is lawful; and though we have an aversion to it, we are bound to accept, and pretend to make use of it.

If one be sitting by the fire, great care must be had of spitting into it, upon the brands, or into the chimney; much less is he to play the fool with tongs, or employ himself in putting the sticks together; but if the person visited shows any inclination to mend the fire, he is obliged, in that case, to seize upon the tongs, to ease him of that trouble, unless the person of honor seems desirous to do it himself for his own recreation.

Being set by the fire, it is not commendable to rise up from his seat and turn his back to the chimney; but if the person of quality rises, he is bound to rise also.

If by accident there be but one screen in the room where you are with the said person, and you be constrained to make use of it, after some formal reluctancy, you must take it, but so as to take opportunity (as soon as you can without his perceiving it) and lay it privately by.

[A screen is defined as, "a device to keep off the wind or the heat of the fire." This was probably a partition of some kind that, when he was too warm, a person could step behind and cool off a bit.]

If upon any occasion a person of that quality happens to be at your house, and sitting to the fire, you must not suffer any of your servants to present him with a screen but do it civilly yourself.

If it so happens that you be alone together, and the candle be to be snuffed, you must do it with the snuffers, not your fingers, and that neatly and quick, lest the person of honor be offended with the smell.

As for women, it is [as] immodest for them to have their coats pinned up by the fire, as to walk with them tucked up in the streets.

When we are talking, it is not civil to use odd or much gesture with our hands; it implies ordinarily, they have but little to say, whose elegance lies not in the motions and contortions of the body.

But being in discourse with a man, it is no less than ridiculous to pull him by the buttons, to play with the band-strings, belt, or cloak; or to punch him now and then on the stomach; it is a pleasant sight, and well worthy of laughter to see him that is so punched, fall back and retire; while the other insensible of his absurdity, pursues and presses him into some corner, where he is at last glad to cry quarter, before his comrade perceives he is in danger.

It argues neglect, and to undervalue a man, to sleep when his is discoursing or reading; therefore good manners command it to be forbid: besides, something there may happen in the act that may offend, as snoring, sweating, gaping, or dribbling.

It is unbecoming, likewise, to accustom ourselves to make mouths, to loll out our tongue, to roll it in our mouths, to bite our lips, to play with our mustaches, to pull out our hairs, to twinkle with our eyes, to clap or rub our hands violently for joy, to pull out our fingers, to snap them one after another; to scratch or shrug with our shoulders as if there were creepers upon our back.

109

It is not becoming to break into violent and loud laughter upon any occasion whatever; and worse to laugh always without any occasion.

Fatuus in risu exaltat vocem suam; vir autem sapiens vix tacite ridebit. Ecc. c. 21.

In discourse be very careful to avoid insignificant, frivolous, or affected words, and land-stories, which are generally known and pass among old wives and children: these expose us to contempt and censure; and by the rarities we produce, others may guess at the furniture of our closet.

Be not in your discourse fond to discover your academical learning, nor use philosophical terms, nor ends of Latin, to be esteemed by them that understand not. And of this young scholars are guilty, that have more confidence than prudence. The best way to discourse is on all occasions to speak candidly and fairly for truth's sake, not vain glory.

If the person we are entertaining lets anything fall, we are obliged on that, and any such occasion, to stoop suddenly and take it up, and not suffer them to do it themselves.

If they sneeze, we must not cry out, "God bless you," with any considerable loudness, but pull off our hat, make our reverence, and speak that benediction to ourselves.

If it happens he wants anyone of his servants that is not ready at hand, it is our duty to call them, not aloud at the top of the stairs or at the window, but to find them out where they are, and let them know their lord calls them: and indeed, among intelligent persons, it is looked upon to the diminution of the master and mistress, where servants are permitted to call for anything aloud, or to deliver their messages out of the window or from the top of the stairs; for it implies the servant has no discretion nor respect for them; and the master and mistress, indeed, are not worthy of it; not having the wit to conserve a reverence in their servants by restraining them from those acts of incivility and laziness.

We must be always very attentive to what they say, lest we put them to the trouble of speaking things twice; we must not interrupt them while they are speaking, but expect till they have done before we give them our answer. We must have great care how we contradict them; and if necessity obliges us to inform them of the truth, we must first beg their excuse, and if they persist in their error, we are not to contend, but give over till some better occasion.

When it comes to our turn to speak, we are not to entertain them with things we do not understand at all, or imperfectly.

1 Si eſt tibi intellectus, reſponde proximo: fin autem ſit manus tua ſuper os tuum, ne cupiaris in verbo indiſciplinato, & confundaris. Eccl. cap. 5

If we be in company more learned, or fitter for discourse, we must leave it to them, hear them

2 Adoleſcens loquere in tua cauſa vix, quum neceſſe fuerit, ſi bis interrogatus fueris, habeas caput tuum reſponſum ſuum. In multis eſto quaſi inſcius, & audi tacens, ſimul & quærens. Id. cap. 32.

attentively, and be silent; or if we be pressed to speak our judgments, we must do it short, in few words; and have a particular care of imitating their indiscretion who affect to have the whole talk at the table, and when their mouth is once open, can never shut it again.

1 Nec verò tanquam in poſſeſſionem ſuam venerit, dit Ciceron d'un grand parieur, excludat alios; ſed cum reliquis juribus, tum in ſermone, communi viciſſitudine nonnunquam utendum putet. Offic. lib. 1.

Reservedness is by some esteemed a virtue; but certainly, to me, it appears the symptom of a sullen and stupid nature, and unwelcome to all societies, when a hearty communicative man is useful and acceptable.

Freedom has its latitude, and discretion should limit it and allot it its degrees, according to your own kindness and the obligation to the person. Nor is it prudence to let a man at first sight perceive all that is within you. There may be discontent, vice, or infirmity at the bottom.

To be over-bold and rushing into discourse before our superiors is as great an error as to interrupt them in it, or to deny them place or respect.

Use not frequently in discourse the names of God or Devil, nor Scripture; this is not only sinful, but indecent.

Be not nasty in your clothes nor body, as in sweating, belching, biting your nails, rubbing your teeth, or picking your ears or nose. To keep your hands in your pockets is like a lout [an awkward, stupid person].

If one be obliged to complement any person, he must do it as short as is possible, and return his answers rather in congees [departing statements] than any prolonged discourse.

If this great person makes us put on our hats (which is not to be done without particular command), we are to pull them off again upon mention of him and of his relations, or any person of principal dignity allied, or in any way intimate with the Grandee with whom we are in discourse; but if by pulling them off often, we find ourselves troublesome to him, and are forbidden again, it is then manners to keep them on.

In all our converse we are carefully to refrain [from] swearing, it being a vice into which many people fall by an ill habit; supposing it vainly an elegance, and great ornament to their discourse; and when we forbid swearing, we intend to exclude all little and trifling oaths with the rest, which signify nothing; this being certain, neither the one nor the other are signs of good education; for when one swears before a person of honor (if there were no worse sentence to follow), he may be justly pronounced a clown.

On the contrary, we ought to be plain and modest in our discourse, so as he may take notice of our retention, and the respect we would persuade him we have for his person.

For which reason it is to be thought great incivility to question and interrogate a person of honor, or any other, about trifling and impertinent things, unless they be our servants, or some other people under our authority. Again, if one be obliged to press anything from such a person, it is to be done with such caution and civility as may encourage him to answer. As for example, if you would know whether he would be in the campaign this summer, we must not cry bluntly, "Sir, will you go into the Army?" That would be too irreverent and familiar; but we must say, "I do not question, Sir, if your health or affairs will permit, but you will be in the field this summer?" and in that case there is no offence but your curiosity, which is excusable when accompanied with respect.

We have said before that nature has given us rules for our modesty, and they ought, indeed, to serve for our discourse also, it being great disrespect to speak the least immodest word before any, but more especially persons of honor. In the company of women, it is not commendable to use equivocation, or ambiguity of expression, being an intrenchment upon civility and modest converse.

* Semper abftinendum eft à verbis unde fit verecordia. *Sen.*

Avoid the recital of such things as will make others blush, or that reflect ignominiously on any, unless you know them very well, and your company especially. No good man but will avoid repeating anything that is profane, or playing with Scripture, in distorting the sense, or making it into ridicule.

And not only equivocal words, but such likewise as leave, or may leave the least idea or image of immodesty in the minds of the hearers.

And as oaths, and licentiousness in discourse, are repugnant to civility, so contention, choler [anger], hyperboles, rodomontades [boasting], lies, reproaches, self-applauses by disparaging others, magnifying himself with perpetual repetitions of his own prudence, as "I would not have done this, I could not do that;" whereby designing to insinuate his own justice and discretion, he becomes troublesome and makes himself ridiculous.

115

But if they who talk much and long, and yet speak nothing to the purpose; if they who cannot speak fix words without an apology of half an hour; if they who are ready to quarrel, and pull their adversary by the beard in every argument they entertain, though the thing be never so indifferent; if those who never speak but in a heat, and run out into passion, though no occasion be given; if all these, I say, be absurd, those who cannot speak but in such a tone as puts their auditory into a fit of the megrim [gives them a headache], are deservedly much more; wherefore all these imperfections are to be particularly avoided: and last of all, one is to have respect to his natural voice, and to raise or depress it according to his distance from the person with whom he is in discourse; which distance ought to be our direction, unless the person be deaf, and in that case we are allowed to exceed.

Another rudeness there is which is too frequent, among such as never think they are heard, unless they come up so close to your face, as to run against your nose; in that case you are to pray heartily their breath may be sweet, or you're a dead man.

Furthermore, we are to observe our visits be not too long, and that if the person of honor does not dismiss us himself, we be sure to take our opportunity when he is silent, when he calls for anybody else, or gives in intimation of business otherwhere: in that case we may depart without much ceremony; and if a third person come in, and the discourse be addressed to him, we may withdraw without speaking a word.

If he perceives our retreat, and the great person will do us the honor to accompany us out of the chamber, we must not oppose, that would imply we thought he did not understand what he was doing; and perhaps we should hinder him from doing what he intended not for us. We are only to testify by some little formality, that if that honor be directed to us, we do not think ourselves worthy; and this is to be done as we are passing forwards, without looking behind us, or else turning back, and stopping to let him pass, as presuming he has business that way in some other place.

If while we are in the presence of this person of honor, another person should come in superior to us, thought inferior to the person with whom we are in discourse; we are not to quit the person with whom we were before, to address ourselves to the new comer, but give him only some silent token of our respect. If the newcomer be of quality superior to the person to whom we made the visit, in that case (as it is to be supposed, the person we visit, will address himself according to his duty) so we, behaving ourselves accordingly, are to leave the first to do honor to the last.

If the person of quality entertains discourse with another, we are not to take advantage, and to fall a talking to our next neighbor; it would be unhandsome to talk so loud as to disturb him; and to whisper would be suspicious, and make him think you wcrc talking something of him.

If the grand person be going out of the room, either in his house, or our own, we are bound (if there be space) to get before him if we can, to hold up the hangings, and open the doors for him, though there be servants by, it being a great testimony of reverence and respect.

Chapter 7
Demeanor in the Church

At our entrance into the church (at least the quire or body of it) we are obliged to make a profound reverence; and composing ourselves with as much modesty as we may, pass on to our seats: If any be so unhappy as to forget, or so insolently profane as to despise it out of respect to the place, yet he ought to do it in civility to the persons of honor which are generally there; but indecorums in holy places are looked upon as effects of ill education, according to the principles established before, and received all the world over, that our actions are to be conformed according to the circumstances of time, and the place where we are; and for that cause we are to stand, sit, or kneel, according to the directions of the rubric, and the practice of the rest of the congregation. For example, we sit at the Psalms, the first and second lessons, and the Epistles; we stand up at the Gospel and the Creed, and kneel at all the rest of the service; but more especially when we receive the Communion.

It is not decent to make faces or mouths when we are at our devotions, to say our prayers loud, or to mumble them so over, as to give disturbance to those who sit next [to us].

We must sit still and be silent at sermon.

In private chapels where persons of honor are present, it is not proper to sit down, but to stand up until the text be named.

If one be to lead a woman to church, or otherwhere, he must lead her in his right hand, putting her next to the wall as he walks, and above him in the pew, observing still when he leads her, to have his glove upon his hand. For when one gives his hand to a lady, either there, or in any other place, it is a general rule he must do it with his glove on. He is likewise to enter everywhere before her to open the doors, and make place for her; but if it happens there be persons of greater quality to lead her, he is to deliver her hand to them, and not keep it from anybody, unless the lady commands him expressly, or he be assured the person to take it will be dissatisfied thereby.

The woman is likewise to take notice, that it is not only vanity, but inexcusable arrogance to cause herself to be led, or her train carried up in the church, where God Himself is more particularly, and more effectually present.

Chapter 8
How to Walk with Great Persons, and the Manner of Greeting

If we be to walk in the streets, and to discourse with any person of honor, as we go along with him, we are always to observe to give him the upper hand, and not to keep exactly side by side with him, but a little behind, unless when he speaks to us, and we step forward to give him our answer, and that is to be done uncovered.

If while we are walking we meet with any person of our acquaintance, or see any man's footman pass by that we know, we must have a care of calling out after them, "You Boy! How does your master? My service to your lady," etc. There is nothing more clownish; nor must we leave the person we are walking with, to run to them, but if we have business with them, and are not at that time in discourse with the person of quality, we may make a private sign to them to come to us, and stealing back, deliver what we have to say quickly, and return; otherwise we may salute them at a distance, so as the person of quality need not perceive it.

If one walk with this person of quality in a chamber or walk, he must always place himself beneath him. In a chamber where the bed stands, is the upper end, if there be one in it; if not, we are to regulate ourselves by the door. If it be in a garden, we must be sure to keep the left hand, and without affectation or trouble to him, recover that side at every turn.

If there be three walking together, the middle is the most honorable place, and belongs to the best man in the company; the right hand is next, and the left the third.

But this is generally observable, that walking two and two, at the end of every walk we must be sure to turn towards the person with whom we are walking, and not outwards, lest we be guilty of turning our backs upon him.

If the person of honor sits down, and has a mind to repose, we and other persons being by, it would be ridiculous for us to walk on, and leave him alone to his rest, if we pretend the least difference in the world.

If we meet any person of condition in the street, or elsewhere, we must always give him the wall; or if there be no such thing to direct us, we must pass by his left hand still, to leave his right hand at liberty; and this rule is an authentic among coaches.

If we be to salute any person arrived lately out of the country, it must be done with an humble inflexion of our bodies, taking off our glove, and putting our hand down to the ground; but above all, we are not to do it precipitously, nor with over much pains, neither throwing ourselves hastily upon our nose, nor rising up again too suddenly, but gently and by degrees, lest the person saluted bowing at the same time to you, might have his teeth beaten out by the throwing up [of] your head.

If it be a lady of quality, we are not to salute her unless she presents herself in civility, and then only in appearance by putting our faces to her hood; but whether we salute her or not, our reverence must be performed with low and decent inclination of the body.

If in the company of the said lady, there happens to be others of equal condition, and independent upon her; but if they be dependent, and of much inferior rank, it is uncivil to salute them, and treat them equally with their superiors: yet they are not to be saluted unless they be of your acquaintance, unless they be presented to you.

Chapter 9
How to Behave in Congratulations and Condolements with Great Persons, and of the Neatness and Propriety of Our Clothes

If we understand a person for whom we have any respect has any occasion to rejoice, or be sad, civility requires we conform ourselves in such sort, that he may be persuaded of our affection and concernment for his affairs.

The neatness and property of our clothes may be said to show a great part of our breeding, it being a great discovery of the discretion of the persons by them; for how is it possible to see a man ridiculous in his habit, but we must presently conclude he himself is ridiculous?

Property I call a certain suitableness and convenience between the clothes and the person, as civility is the framing and adapting our actions to the satisfaction of other people; and if we desire to be exact, we must proportion them to our shape, our condition, and age.

The contrary to this property is unsuitableness, which consists in too much exactness or direct carelessness, and is the fault of such as are vain, or too well conceited of themselves, or else of such as are too little and therefore negligent, lazy, slovenly, or morose.

Some there are that are so little concerned for their apparel that their care therein extends no further than just necessity. They matter not decency, so that they may be defended against the injuries of the weather. Certainly, he that goes to dine with a friend in foul linen, prefers the filling of his stomach before the satisfaction of his friend, and comes in love to nobody but his own belly.

These two faults are each of them to be condemned; but that which proceeds from sordidness or neglect is the worst of the two; for besides that, it gives a character to the man, as well as the other; it disobliges the person before whom we appear; as if we did not value his opinion of us, or thought him unworthy to be visited with better.

But the best rule we can observe for the fashion of our clothes is the mode; to that it is we must submit all our own fancy and reason; observing still what is generally worn, and following their fashion without further dispute.

This mode hath likewise two faults of excess, the one is singularity, the other is profusion, both one and the other making one ridiculous.

And indeed if a person, how modest or reserved soever he be, would be obstinate, and endeavor to oppose the torrent of the fashion appearing; for example, in a high crowned hat, when they wear low, he would run a hazard of being followed by the boys, and admired like one of the sights in Bartholomew Fair.

The other extreme is profusion, which consists in out doing the mode; as if when breeches are worn an ell wide at the knees, one should have made his two; if a lady's train should be half an ell long, another should make hers twice as much; if some knots of ribband be worn at the side of the knees, a third will have them up to his pocket holes; and all things so inconveniently suitable, his very knots for his shoes shall be a foot long or more. [An ell is a unit of measurement originally understood to be the same as a cubit, the length between the elbow and the tip of the middle finger on the outstretched hand. Many nations had different lengths of ells. The French ell was fifty-four inches. In England it was usually forty-five inches. These measurements, however, do not seem to fit the above description of clothing.]

To avoid this incommodious extravagancy, we must address ourselves to the court, which is the source and foundation of fashions, and follow in this, (as well as in other things which depend upon fancy) the example of the soberest and most moderate men.

For this reason, those who are too remote, or unable by any other impediment to go to court themselves, are to gain acquaintance, if they can, with some prudent person who is frequently there; and by his pattern or direction, order his clothes, with reference as near as may be to his quality, age, and estate: and this person whom he is to make his model, ought in my judgement not only to be familiar at court, but to have some kind of wit and contrivance of his own; for they who are such will retrench a great part of the luxury of a fashion, and reduce it to suit with his convenience and modesty, which ought to be the principal grounds of a Christian's conduct, as we have hinted before in the beginning of this treatise.

We have said before, our habits ought to be adapted to our conditions; and it is easy to judge of the truth of that rule if we imagine a churchman (for example) habiting himself in the dress of a layman (or at least as near as he can) for who is there would think he was right in his wits, or that he was not in masquerade, or going a mumming [masquerading] to some person of his acquaintance, and so of the rest.

So it is likewise as to our age, for an old man or woman to spruce themselves up like people of fifteen, is as abominably improper as to make a merry feast at a funeral.

But to proportion their clothes to their bodies, is a thing few persons observe, and yet very essential to their being neat and becoming; and indeed without that, we do but make ourselves ridiculous: from hence it is requisite, when clothes are worn generally very large, they be made lesser for little men; otherwise a little man would be lost in a great band (because it was the fashion) and a great broad brimmed hat would be thought to walk alone, if he should wear it upon his head; and would be no less ridiculous than a painter, who should so far transgress the rules of art, as to make great arms to a little picture, or little legs to a great.

This agreeableness therefore ought to be exact and adequate both to age, person, and condition, avoiding extremities on both sides, and being neither too much out of the fashion, nor in.

And it is not only the decency and aptitude of the clothes which give a character of a person, but his servants, his equipage, his house, his furniture, and his table; all these ought to be modeled and proportioned to his quality, for they are all of them so many mouths declaring the wit or weakness of their master; besides extravagance in that nature is a more than ordinary means to make people deficient in their respects to other people, by elating their minds, and disposing them to vanity and disdain.

The second part of this property or decency is neatness, which is the more necessary, because it supplies the other when it is defective; for if one's clothes be neat, and linen clean, it matters not whether they be rich and magnificent, a man shall always be respected though his condition be but mean.

With all these, it is convenient to keep one's head combed, his eyes and teeth washed and clean, otherwise his negligence spoils his mouth, and his breath offends every man he talks with; we ought likewise to cut our nails constantly, both on our fingers and toes, and take such course in all things, as to give no cause of disgust to the people with whom we converse.

Chapter 10
Observations at the Table

If it so happens that the person of quality we have hitherto proposed detains you to dine with him, it is uncivil to wash with him unless you be commanded expressly; if there be no servant by to take away the napkin when he has wiped, the person invited must take it from him, and not suffer it to continue in his hands.

He must be sure to stand up at grace.

Grace being said, he is to stand still till he be placed, or dispose himself at the lower end of the table. When he is set, he must keep himself uncovered till the rest sit down, and the person of quality has put on his hat.

He must keep his body straight upon his chair, and not lay his elbows upon the table.

In taking or giving seats at table, a chair with arms is more honorable than [one] with [a] back only, and those than stools.

In eating, observe to let your hands be clean. Feed not with both your hands. Don't keep you knife in your hand. Dip not your fingers in the sauce, nor lick [them] when you have done [so]. Wipe your mouth and keep your spoon clean. If you are desired to carve for anyone, be sure to touch no part of it, if possible, with your fingers. Gnaw not bones, nor handle dogs, nor sprawl upon the floor; and if you have occasion to sneeze or cough, take your hat, or put your napkin before your face. Drink not with your mouth full or unwiped, nor so long till you are forced to breathe into the glass. Talk not at table of anything that may be ungrateful or impertinent; and lastly, avoid anything that may interrupt the cheerfulness of the company.

He must not by any ravenous gesture discover he is hungry, nor fix his eyes too greedily upon the meat, as he would devour it all himself.

He must have a care his hand be not first in the dish, unless he be desired to help his neighbors.

If he be entreated to carve, he must give the best pieces away, leave the rest, and touch nothing but with his fork; for which reason, if the person of quality desired to be carved, it would be convenient for the person invited to understand how to carve neatly and methodically, and how to choose the best bits, that he may be able to serve him with advantage.

For example, if it be chicken broth, and he be entreated to help him with a piece of the chicken that is usually served up in it; the breast is the best part, the wings and legs are the next. Of a green goose, the leg being first cut off as little as may be, the best piece is the wing drawn down all along the breast and apron. Of a loin of veal, the bones next to the rump [are best]. And of them the general opinion is, as in all boiled fowl, the legs are the best.

In all fowl for the spit, all persons pretending to any knowledge in that kind, or that are anything curious in their meats, do agree, that of such as scratch the earth with their claws, the wings are better than the legs. As on the contrary, the legs are better in such as fly aloft in the air, and the partridge being none of that sort, must be by consequence be reckoned among the other; that is, of all water fowl anyway certainly the leg is best, and of all other fowl, except pheasants, capons, pullets, and partridge. It hath been a discourse oftentimes concerning what are properly fowl, and what birds, and concluded that those that carry meat to their young are birds, and those fowl that carry their young to their meat.

In carving, it is proper to give of teal, woodcock, partridge, and fowl of that bigness a leg and wing to one person, and the body and other leg and wing together to another, and not divide it to serve three.

In the season when fowl lay eggs, the body and eggs are the best part, and preferred.

Pigeons' rumps, woodcocks' heads, pigs' strunt [tail or rump], neck of a rabbit, and the soul [liver] of a goose are particular curiosities, that are rather left to them that fancy them to take themselves, than to be offered. It is not civil to take a woodcock's head to yourself, because they are usually left, and sent to be broiled and generally liked of. The piece between the wing and the leg of a cygnet is the best part about it.

The most ordinary way of cutting up a roast fowl is by cutting off the four principal members, beginning first with the legs.

If the fowl be of the larger sort, as turkeys, geese, or the like, the best part to carve to the best in the company is the piece from the wing to the breast, observing always to cut it long ways towards the rump.

As to common meat, there are few ignorant of the best pieces; so that it will be to no purpose to insert them here, the design of this book being to treat of such things as are not commonly known; so that not to deviate from my intention, I shall only set down by the by.

That of boiled beef, the part which is most interlarded with fat and lean, is the best; and the short ribs being usually most tender, is to be preferred before any other.

A leg of mutton is cut above the handle, by thrusting the knife as deep into it as one may to bring out the gravy and the joint on the other side is a little bone fit to be presented, and the pope's eye.

A shoulder of mutton is to be cut like a semicircle between the flap and the hand.

In a suckling pig, the part most approved by such as are dainty, is the ears and the skin. In hares, leverets, and rabbits, the most esteemed pieces (called by way of excellence, the huntsman's piece) is by the sides of the tail, and next to that is the back, legs, and wings [shoulders or ribs perhaps?].

In fish, the *virtuosi* are of opinion, the head, and what is near about it, is generally the best: whence it is, at a well-ordered table the head of the fish (if there be any) is set at the upper end; and so it is of the porpoise, fresh salmon, pike, or carp; in which last, it is to be observed the tongue is always the best bit.

In fish which have but one long bone running down their backs, as the sole, etc. the middle is to be carved without dispute, as being the best without contradiction. However, in reaching any of soles, flounders, place, or the like; if they are so large in their kind as not to be given whole, the tail half is the best.

It is to be observed that to touch fish (unless it be in paste) with a knife, is not handsome, being rather to be taken up with our fork and spoon, and laid neatly upon a plate, presented as is desired.

It has been formerly the custom to crack and peel such fruits as were hollow, as nuts, etc. And it is yet observed, too, at all great tables to bring up walnuts cracked and peeled.

Walnuts and such fruit are taken out of the dish with one's hand, without further ceremony in the same manner as dry sweet meats.

Olives are to be taken out of the dish with a spoon, and not the fork, which mistake I have seen the occasion of very good laughter.

All sorts of tarts, wet sweet meats, and cake, being cut first upon the dish in which they were served up are to be taken up at the point of our knives, laid dexterously upon a plate, and presented.

It is to be observed, if you be desired to help anyone with anything [that] is to be carved, [or] with a spoon; you must call for another [utensil] and not make use of your own if you have used it before. If you have not used it before, it is to be presented with the plate unless the person who desired you to help him sent his own spoon along with it. Whatever you carve is to be presented upon a clean plate, and by no means either upon your fork, your knife's point, or your spoon.

To give anything from your own plate to another to eat of, though he be an inferior, favors of arrogance, much less an apple or a pear that has been bitten by you before. Have a care likewise of blowing froth from off a cup, or any dust from roasted apples or toast; for the proverb says, "there is no wind but there is some rain." [You might accidently spit on someone.]

If the person to whom you present your plate be near you, the best way is to deliver it yourself, pulling off your hat as you present it first to him, but no more afterwards for fear of giving him trouble.

If one be unhandy at carving, his best way will be to excuse himself.

If you be carved, it is but civil to accept whatever is offered, pulling off your hat still when it is done by a superior.

It is not handsome to ask for anything one's self, especially if it be a dainty; and it would show little breeding, if when one is offered his choice of several things, he should take the best: the usual answer in that case is, "which you please."

To be nice and curious at the table is indecent; as likewise to cry aloud, "I can eat none of this, I can eat none of that; I love no roast, I eat no rabbit; I cannot endure pepper, nutmeg, or onion."

It is very uncivil in anyone that is a guest at a friend's table to find fault or discommend anything that is not agreeable to him. Desire not any man to smell to such a thing, because you apprehend it stinks; but rather say, "Do not smell, it is not right."

These being but imaginary aversions corrected easily by their friends when they were young, or by themselves now, if they would constrain themselves, endure a little hunger, and not dote and indulge their appetites as they do; and therefore those kind of repugnances are to be concealed as much as they can; if we be carved with anything we do not like, we must receive it however, and though our disgust be many times invincible, and it would be tyranny to require we should eat what we nauseate; yet it is but civil to accept it, though we let it lie till we have an opportunity of changing our plate without being observed.

If every man helps himself, we must have a care our hand be not in the dish before the person of quality's, and be sure to carve only on that side with is next to us; much less ought we to take the best piece, though it falls to our share to be the last. What we take, we must take at once; it is not civil to eat out of the dish bit by bit.

Care must likewise be had of reaching over the dishes with our arms to come at another we like better.

It is likewise to be observed we are to wipe our spoon every time we put it into the dish. Some people being so delicate, they will not eat after a man has eaten with his spoon and not wiped it.

If we be at table with persons of more than ordinary neatness, it is not sufficient to wipe our spoon, but we must lay it by and call for another when we have done; it being the mode at present to give clean spoons with every plate, and spoons on purpose for sauce.

Be we as hungry as we may, we must not gormandize [to eat gluttonously], nor eat so fast as we would choke ourselves. We must close our lips when we eat, and not smack like a pig, or make any other noise. [It is] ungrateful to the company. Much less are we to keep a clutter, clattering the dishes against one another, grating our knives against the plates, or rubbing them as if they would never be clean. These are as so many signals, giving the alarm to the company, and disposing them to the observation of our voracity, of which, perhaps, otherwise they would have never taken notice.

Pottage is not to be eaten out of the dish. We are to take it upon our plates and if it be too hot, not blow it in our spoon, as some do very indecently, but have patience till it cools of itself.

If one happens by accident to burn himself, he must conceal it if he can; but if it be too hot to be endured, as it falls out sometimes, he must quickly, before it be perceived, take his plate in one hand, and hiding himself with the other, and spitting it into the plate, give it presently away to the servant behind him. Civility requires a man should be cleanly; but it does not oblige a man to *felo de se*. [Or kill himself. *Felo de se* is Latin for "felon of him- or herself", and was a concept applied against the assets of adults who committed suicide. Early English common law, among others, considered suicide a crime. If a person was found guilty of it, their estates would be charged penalties including forfeiture of property to the monarch and a shameful burial.]

We must not bite our bread but cut or break it as we put it to our mouths, and be sure not to keep the knife in our hands, it being as unhandsome as when we eat pears or plums to put it to our mouths with them.

We must cut our meat into small pieces and not take them so big into our mouths that they may make our cheeks stick out like satchels on each side as we are eating.

We must not gnaw the bones with our teeth, make a noise, or stir to break them, nor shake, or suck them to come at the marrow. We must cut our meat upon our plates in small pieces and eat it afterwards cleanly.

We must be cautious of dipping or sopping in the dish or carrying our meat to the salt cellar every mouthful. We must rather take our salt upon the point of our knives, and the sauce in a spoon, and lay them both upon our plates.

We must not hang too much over our plate with our bodies, nor let half we intend to our mouth fall short upon our bands [ties].

There is nothing more unbecoming than to lick one's fingers, knife, spoon, or fork, to wipe his plate or dish bottom with his fingers, to drink up the porridge, sauce or gravy, or pour it out upon one's plate; none of which can be done, but with the derision of the whole company. It is to be observed when our fingers, knife, fork, or anything else if foul, we are to wipe them with our napkins, and by no means with the tablecloth. Grease not your napkin too much so as to nauseate your neighbor.

When you have blown your nose in your handkerchief, look not into it as if there were a jewel dropped out of your head.

It is requisite to consider well when a glass comes in health to a person of great quality, how far your acquaintance will permit you to use it with familiarity and respect: whether to say aloud, "My lord, your lordship's good health," or only to your neighbor, "Sir, my lord N.'s good health."

Though it be customary, yet it favors rather of formality and ignorance to stop in the middle of your discourse because one in the company is drinking. With good manners you may proceed in your story, though not to ask a man a question; for any man may hear, though not speak in his drink.

If at any time your own health is begun, it is requisite to observe the company; for it they are inferiors, it is civil to be uncovered as well as they.

Avoid carefully all wrangling or occasion of anger at table, though a fault be committed there by your servants, refer it rather till afterwards; for the board as well as the bed should be the place for reconciling, rather than fomenting of difference.

If ever you are desired to help another, you must always cut him in the best place rather than the worst.

If one be to return a knife, fork, or spoon which was lent him, he must either wipe it on his napkin, or send it to the cupboard to be made clean, and then calling for a clean plate, deliver it civilly back to the person who lent it.

If it happens by any accident extraordinary, a man has anything in his mouth which he cannot get down, it would be very unseemly to let it fall out suddenly upon his plate as if he had vomited. He must rather spit it into his hand, and convey it privately upon his plate, which he is to give away immediately if he can, so as no notice may be taken, and be sure never to spit anything out upon the ground.

To blow one's nose upon one's napkin, or if openly upon his handkerchief, to snuff, or hawk, or bring up anything from the bottom of one's stomach are things ill favored. They are abominable to all the world. We must abstain from them by all means if we can; if not, do them as privately as possible, by covering our faces with our hats, or otherwise.

We must not on the other side simper and mince but eat freely and civilly as we have occasion. We must not however appear insatiable, but contain and leave off with the first, unless the person of quality (whose civility obliges him not to suffer the meat to be taken away till everybody has done eating) encourage us to freedom.

It is not civil likewise during the repast to criticize or find fault with the meat or sauces, or to trouble himself and company with perpetual discourses of belly-timber [food], that being a sure sign of an epicure, and one ill provided of better discourse.

As one is not to eat along, and by stealth, so he is not to drink in company sneakingly of anything not intended for him.

It is unhandsome to call first for drink till the persons of quality have drunk before you.

It is not answerable to the respect we owe to call aloud for beer or for wine. We must rather speak low to the officer or lacquey behind us; or if they be out of distance to hear, make signs to them to come.

It is gross incivility to begin any person of honor's health, and to address it to himself.

If another person begins it in gallantry, it is your duty to pledge him; but you must do it without signifying it to the person himself; which is to be done in this manner, speaking to the person to whom you drink; "Sir, my service to you, a good health to my lord;" and not (as is frequent) "my lord, your lordship's good health, and I carry it to my master."

It is a very great absurdity in speaking to any noble person to call him by his name, or drinking his lady's health (or any of his relations) to him, to say, "Sir, a good health to my lady your wife," or "to my lord your brother." But we must name her by the quality of her husband, and the rest either by their surnames or their titles; as thus, "To my Lady Duchess," if her husband be a duke, or "To my Lord Marquess, your brother," if his brother be so. If we be speaking, or to answer a person of honor, and at the same time he puts the glass to his mouth to drink, we are to stop, and be silent till he has done, and then proceed in our discourse.

It favors too much of familiarity to sip our wine and make two or three draughts of a glass. We must drink it gravely at once, with our eyes in the glass (not staring about the room) and be sure our mouth be not full; I say gravely and deliberately, lest guggling [gulping] it down too fast, we should be forced to bring it up again, which would be a great rudeness, and nauseate the whole table. Besides, throwing it down our throats as into a tunnel would be an action more fit for a juggler than a gentleman.

We must have a care after we have drunk, of fetching any loud sighs, as if our breath was gone in the draught, so as the whole company may perceive it.

It is not well to receive your drink nor meat, nor ought that you call for, on that side next to the person of honor; for those who are accurately bred, receive it generally on the other.

If the person of honor drinks a health to you, or your own, you must be sure to be uncovered, inclining forward till he has drunk, and not pledge him without precise order.

If he speaks to you, you must likewise be uncovered till you have answered him and have special care you mouth be not full. The same respect is to be shown him whenever he speaks, till he expressly forbids it; after which you arc to be covered, lest he be incommoded.

It is not civil to rub your teeth before people, nor at meals, or after to pick them with your knife or fork; for that is a thing both indecent and distasteful.

It is not handsome likewise to wash one's mouth or gargle after meals before persons of honor.

If one rises from the table before the rest, he must pull off his hat, and have somebody ready behind him to take away his napkin and plate, they being no handsome land-skip when he is gone; neither would his familiarity be laudable, who if no servant was there, should rise, and not take them away himself.

When the plates are changed, we must not suffer the servants which deliver the clean plates to begin with us, but attend till the person of honor and the rest of our superiors be served, especially the ladies to whom (if we observe the servants remiss) we are with a bow to make a present of our own.

If a prince or princess desires your presence at any collation or regale, you must not sit down at the table, but place yourself behind their chair, to be ready to present them with plates or drink as they have occasion. If it be a prince, and he commands you to sit down, you may do it at the lower end of the table; but if it be a princess, it shows more breeding and respect to desire to be excused.

Chapter 11
How to Behave When a Noble Person Visits, and When to Make Returns

If the said person of quality shall do us the honor to make us a visit and we have notice he is arrived, it is our duty to run immediately out and receive him at his coach, or at least as far as we can.

If he surprises us in our chamber, we must rise up from our seats, quit all the business we were about, and apply ourselves forthwith to the paying our respects, which we are to continue (without any avocation whatever) till he departs. If he finds us in bed, we must remain as he found us till he goes away.

But in some cases there is a mediocrity to be observed; for if the person of honor shall please to dispense with our ceremonies so far, as to command us to desist, we ought not in manners to persevere, seeing nothing can give stronger testimony of his authority and dominion in a house, than submission and obedience to the master.

And we are to observe that it is not only to persons of honor to whom we are obliged to pay the civility of our house, but to everyone else which comes to us under the character of a stranger. If a person of honor makes us a visit, though he has no priority but in years, yet in that respect we are bound to give him precedence, the upper end of the table, and use him with the same respect (proportionably) as the best qualified person of all.

For this reason, if a person of that quality makes us a visit in civility, it will be a bad return to make him attend long before we come to him, unless we be engaged with persons more honorable than he; or be otherwise upon some public affair. In those cases, it is civil to send some gentleman or other qualified person to entertain him till you be at leisure.

When the honorable person has made his visit and retires, we are obliged to wait upon him to his coach; if it be a lady, we are to give her our hand (if there be no person of better quality than us) and having helped her into the coach, we are to continue at the door till her ladyship be gone.

If any young lady be by accident left behind, or goes home another way, it is incumbent upon us to see her safely at home, especially if it be night, or she lives at any distance; and if our own affairs will not permit us to wait on her, we must recommend some other person conduct her.

For the visits we are to return, if we will follow the example, or rather the extravagance of certain people, who consume the greatest part of their lives in visiting others, to oblige them to a return; our best way (as was wittily said) will be to go from door to door. But for a person who knows how to employ his time, and yet is willing to retain a civil correspondence with all people; we must inform him there are some indispensable occasions, in which he cannot without reflection omit making his visits to persons for whom he bears any amity or respect. For example, he is to wait upon a noble person at convenient times, to inform himself of his health, and to continue the good opinion he has of him, and in general, whenever any good or ill accident has given him subject for either sorrow or joy; we are to make our visit in the same dialect, unless we be particularly convinced it will not be welcome.

Chapter 12
Rules to Be Observed in Play
[at Cards or Gambling]

If it should fall out the person of quality obliges us to play (which we must neither propose, nor be too peremptory in denying, if desired) we must by no means show any heat, passion, or impatience to win, they being arguments of a mean spirit and small education. If we cannot command ourselves in them, but find our humor unpleasant and perplexed, our best way is to abstain from it quite, and we shall prevent a thousand inconveniences thereby. On the other side, we ought not to be remiss and negligent in our play nor suffer ourselves to lose compliance, lest we be counted braggadocios for our pains; our losses make us ridiculous, and the person disobliged, as believing we did not think her or him worthy of our intention. Nor is it decent to use any quirks or by-words in your play.

We must not sing or whistle at play so as to give offence or make any noise.

If any difference arises, we are not to be obstinate, but must submit it to judgment; if any trick or foul play be offered, we are not to be presently a top on the house, but tell what we have to say quietly, and prove it as well and as readily as we can.

At all times and in all places swearing is immodest, as we have said before, but especially at play where all things ought to be so carried as not to trouble our diversion.

We must not demand the stakes we win with eagerness or heat; and if anyone has forgotten or failed to put in, we are not rudely to call out, "Pay me my money," or "put in your stake;" but tell them modestly, and in good language, "I won the last stake; somebody has forgotten to [put in their] stake;" and "I have not all [that] I did win."

When one loses, he is always to pay before it be demanded, it being a mark of generosity and nobleness of spirit, to pay what one loses frankly, and without any compunction.

If one knows the person of honor with whom he plays, be over-concerned at his losing. If he wins, he is not to give over till the person of honor leaves off or has recovered his money. If we lose, we must give over quietly when our stock is gone; it being civil enough to conform to our strength, whereas he exposes himself to laughter and contempt who loses more than he has about him to pay.

If the person be passionate at play, we must be cautious of provoking him, but mind our game and not concern ourselves at his words, especially if it be a lady. In that case it is but prudence to take all in good part, and not transgress the serenity of our minds, or the respect we owe unto her.

Yet to conclude this chapter it is best not to play at all, or especially not to love it nor play deep; for it is more chargeable than the seven deadly sins. Yet I would have none so morose as to deny to gratify a lady or a friend within such a compass. Then equanimity in play shows an admirable temper of mind that is fit for anything; but on the contrary, he that insults upon success, or frets upon loss, is always of a passionate and of an uneven disposition, and this as soon as anything will discover the humor of a person.

Chapter 13
Rules to Be Observed at a Ball

If a man finds himself by accident surprised in any assembly or at a Ball, above all things he is to know exactly, I will not say to dance, but the rules and formalities of dancing which are practiced in that place, (for in all countries they are not the same).

If he knows how to dance it is not handsome to be difficult; but if his talent be but indifferent, he must not pretend to over much skill, nor engage himself in dances he does not understand, at least but imperfectly.

If his ear be not good, he is, if possible, to decline it, though he knows his steps never so well; for what can be more ridiculous than to see a man out in his time, and the whole company in confusion by his means; for he might have excused himself, had he pleased, by leading the lady into the middle of the hall, and making a low congee. But he ought first to signify the displeasure he conceived in not being skilled in that excellent recreation, that she might be satisfied it was not contempt or morosity, so much as want of address.

Nihil decet invita, ut ajunt, Minerva, id est, adverfante & repugnante natura. Cic. Off. 1

But if after all our apologies they (for their divertissement) will oblige us to dance, we must by no means refuse; for it is much better to expose ourselves to some little involuntary disorder in being complaisant, than be suspected of pride. In that case we must with as good language as we are able, entreat the lady that she would vouchsafe to dance some dance we conceive we understand, which we must dance afterwards frankly, and as well as we can.

Sin aliquando neceffitas nos ad ea detru-
ferit quæ noftri ingenii non erunt, omnis ad-
hibenda erit cura, meditatio, diligentia, ut
ea, fi non decore, at quàm minimè indecore
facere poffimus: nec tam eft evitandum, ut
bona quæ nobis, data non funt, fequatur,
quàm ut vitia fugiamus. *Cic. lib. Off.*

Having finished our dance, we are to attend that lady to her place, and with a low reverence [bow] take out another: observing when we are taken out again, to return our revenge upon the lady which took us out first, if it be the custom of that place, and by no means to possess ourselves of the seat which belongs to anyone that is dancing.

It is to be observed very strictly likewise, if there be any persons in masquerade, it is uncivil to lay their hand upon their vizards [masks], or to cause them to unmask, unless they have a mind to it themselves. On the contrary, one is obliged to pay more civility to them than to other persons, because many times under those disguises, there are persons of the highest dignity and honor.

Chapter 14
Directions About Singing or Playing Musical Instruments

If one has a faculty of singing, playing upon the music, or making of verses, he must not do anything in company to make it understood; but if it be discovered, and he may be desired to show it in any meeting by a person for whom he bears any respect, he is to excuse himself as modestly as he can. But if his friend persists, it will argue good breeding to sing, play, or repeat his verses without scruple or hesitation; and his prompt and ready obedience shall serve him against censure, whereas a refractory resistance favors of the singing master, and even he is like to have but small doings who thinks to recommend himself by that kind of morosity.

Above all things, he is to have a care of hawking, clearing his throat too much, or being too long in tuning his instrument.

He must be wary also how he commends himself by any fantastical gestures, which imply delight and exceeding satisfaction, or to say when he sings, "Now! This is a good note; hark! This is a better; or observe, this trill, this cadence is excellent."

He must likewise remember to finish as soon as he can that he be not tedious, but leaves the company with an appetite, lest otherwise he should be desired to hold his peace, which notwithstanding, if the person that sings be a gentleman, would be as great an incivility as to have interrupted him by loud talk or discourse.

Chapter 15
Directions Upon the Road in the Coach, on Horseback, or a Hunting

If a person of honor desires our company in a journey he is taking, it is a civil obligation lies upon us to accommodate in all things, never to complain, never to make him stay; to be cheerful, vigorous, and officious in all things; and to imitate them who are never satisfied with their horses, their chambers, their beds, etc. who set their servants one against another, and the master against them all, who are never ready, never satisfied, never in good humor.

And indeed travelling being a kind of warfare, accompanied with cares, diligences, and precautions, as well as with downright labor and fatigue; it is extremely unpleasant, when to all those incommodities is added forwardness and intractability of one's companion; and becomes, indeed, more burdensome then all the rest of the baggage.

If we be to travel by coach, the person of honor is in equity to go in first. After he is set, we are to enter and put ourselves into the lowest place. If the coach be your own, you are to go in the last. The right hand of the hinder part of the coach is the best, the left hand by his side is the next. The third place is over against the person of honor on the other end; and the fourth is by his side. The boots, if there be any, are the lowest, though even there that part which is next to the hinder end is the best.

Being in the coach, we are not to put on our hats but by command, nor to turn our backs upon the person of quality upon any occasion.

It is observable likewise, when we meet with a consecrated host, a procession, funeral, the King, Queen, princes of the blood, or persons of extraordinary dignity, as the Pope's legate, etc. It is a respect due to them for us to stop our coach till they be passed; the men to be uncovered and the ladies to pull off their masks. But if it be the sacrament, we must [get] out of the coach if we can, and [get] down upon our knees, though [it be] in the middle of the street.

If we be to ride, the person of quality is not only to mount first, but we are to hold the stirrup and give him our assistance to get up. As we march, we must observe the same rules as in our walking, that is, to give him the right hand, and keep a little behind him; but if the wind likes so as to carry the dust upon him, we may shift then and dispose of ourselves somewhere else.

We must observe likewise when we come at any river or ford, that it is our office to go first over; but if it falls out by accident we are behind, and must follow the person of quality, it is to be done at such a distance that our horse may not dash nor incommode him any way else.

If he gallops, we must be cautious of galloping before him, nor to gallop and change, or make any parade with our horse, without his order or command.

Again, if we attend him a hunting, we must not outride him, or suffer ourselves to be transported with too much eagerness, but permit him to be first in at the death of the deer; and if he be to be shot down, or cut down with a sword, that honor is to be left for the said person himself.

If by reason of the scarcity of quarters, it falls out that we must lie in the same chamber with the qualified person, we are in civility obliged to let him go first to bed, and afterwards undress ourselves as privately as we can by our own bed, and go to bed too, with care to lie quiet and still, and make no noise in the night that may give him disturbance.

And as we go to bed last, so civility requires we be up first in the morning, that the person of honor may find us dressed when he rises; it being very indecent for us to suffer ourselves to be seen naked, or undressed by a person of quality, our things lying about the room, our bed open, or the chamber, by our means, in any disorder.

It is not decorous to look in the glass to comb, brush or do anything of that nature to ourselves while the said person be in the room, much less to make use of his combs, brushes or anything else that belongs to him.

From hence it is to be concluded how utterly inconsistent it is with all manner of civility, to seize upon the first chamber, the first bed, etc. as soon as ever we come in.

On the other side, it would not suit with the quality of that person, if in an ill place where they are straightened for lodging, he should cause all rashly to be taken up for himself without consideration how others are accommodated. Such an action would not relish of the lord or great person, who to his inferiors has his mutual obligation of courtesy and humanity, and ought to extend it to the sharing in all such inconveniences as are unavoidable.

Chapter 16
Rules in the Writing of Letters

The same exactness and punctuality as is required in our discourse and behavior is to be observed likewise in our letters which are indeed the communication and dialogue of the absent.

To make use of large paper rather than small, and a whole sheet (though we write but six lines in the first page) rather than half a one is no inconsiderable piece of ceremony, one showing reverence and esteem, the other familiarity or indifference.

After "My Lord, Sir," or "Madam," which is usually written at the top before we come to the body of the letter, we are to leave a space or blank, greater or lesser, according to the quality of the person to whom we write.

In the body of the letter, as oft as we have occasion to write "Sir," or "My Lord," (which we are to repeat with respect, especially if what we write has any particular direction to himself, or his affairs) we must do it at length, and not with abbreviation; for example, "you see, Sir, Your Lordship may perceive," and not "Sir," or Your "Lordship."

When we write to any person to whom the titles of Excellence or Highness do equitably belong, we must not only be sure to remember them, but to repeat them as often and as conveniently [as] we may.

If the person to whom we write be not very much above us, we may put the "Sir" under the bottom of the letter in the middle of the space between that and the bottom of the page where you write "your most humble, and most obedient servant." If it be a prince, or any eminent lord, we put "Your Highness," or "Your Lordships," something lower, and "most humble, and most obliged servant," as near the bottom of the page as is possible; which are the most proper epithets to signify our respects, all other importing friendship or familiarity.

And indeed so indecent and unbecoming it is to jumble in any other terms of respect with these, that there is nothing more deformed than to see them confounded; and the rather because errors in that kind make deeper impression than in discourse, where we have the privilege of redressing or excusing them upon the place.

We must have an exact care likewise to preserve an equality in our style; and if the business we write about be serious, to be very cautious of flying out into extravagant, presumptuous, or familiar terms as some people do, who after the first period in a grace and austere style, run out inconsiderately into flashes of wit (as they think) or else into metaphors or high language unfit for any but intimate friends, gallants, or drolls, and contrary to the respect due to a superior, which ought to be insinuated plainly, humbly, and with circumspection.

On the other side, it is no less incongruous if a lord or other great person writes loftily and imperiously though to an inferior; for if that inferior be not of his dependence or a stranger, the person of quality makes himself ridiculous if he writes arrogantly and like a master.

We are to add the day of the month, the year, and the place from whence we write also; for more respect we put them usually at the bottom of our letter on the left hand of our subscription; and indeed to put it at the top when we write to a person of quality is something presumptuous.

For superscribing or directing of letters, you are to observe to an archbishop, or a duke or duchess, "To His Grace" or "Her Grace;" to marquesses, earls, viscounts, and privy counsellors, "the Right Honorable;" to bishops, "To the Right Reverend Father in God;" to ambassadors, or generals, or lord deputies of a kingdom, "His Excellence;" to baronets, knights, bachelors and doctors of divinity and law, "Right Worshipful." If you are to superscribe a letter to an earl or viscount that is beyond the sea, as in France or Flanders, it is better to say only, "These for the Right Honorable My Lord R." etc. because they look upon "My Lord" as a title, and is beyond any count or marquess whatever. All the sons of a duke and marquess are by consent of all, lords, and ought to have the title of "Right Honorable." The eldest sons of earls by the courtesy of England have the same, and commonly carry the title of the barony. To the younger sons of earls, barons, and viscounts, "To the Honorable John B. Esq."

In your letter to any of the quality above you, you are to use the same title as if you were speaking to them. To dukes and archbishops, "Your Grace;" to marquesses, earls, viscounts, barons, "Your Honor" or "Your Lordship." To bishops, "Your Lordship" only. To all countesses, etc. "Your Ladyship" is more proper than "Your Honor," if it be writ from one of quality; but from a servant "Your Honor" is to be observed to his lord or lady.

As it is improper to say "For Mr. B. Esq.", so it is but civil and usual to distinguish between a knight baronet and a knight bachelor; therefore, you must say, "These for Sir N. B. Baronet," but to knights bachelors only the Sir before.

No one superscribes a letter, "For his dear wife," or "loving husband," unless it be one that has not had ingenuous education or have a mind to be laughed at. Because the outside of a letter is to be read by everyone that is not concerned in that interest that is between you: nor is it material to him to be informed that he that writes that letter is such a woman's husband.

If we be desired to abbreviate and spare these ceremonies by writing in a note or ticket, without the great blank at top, or humility at the bottom, we are to obey, rather than be troublesome.

It is not amiss likewise if we take notice, that for greater respect the letter ought to be enclosed in another paper, upon which we are to write the superscription.

Chapter 17
How and When to Expect and Receive Honor, and When It is Not Required

After this instruction, how we are to pay our respects, we cannot conveniently be ignorant of what is due to ourselves, and at what times we are not to expect it. We must know therefore we are not to insist upon any such ceremony in the presence, or in the house of any person of greater quality than we; because civility (as we have said) being always accompanied with humility, exacts it from us to him; and it is according to the order of methods of nature, for the greater to abate and lessen the less: for example, it is indecent for persons of indifferent quality to assume the respect of a higher; as it is for ladies to cause themselves to be led, or to have their trains carried up in the presence, or in the house of any person of much greater quality than themselves.

Chapter 18
Against Such as Are Too Scrupulous

And now in order to our conclusion, it remains I declare, that though for order's sake this treatise is divided into chapters, it follows not that civility is never to be practiced but when such occasions are offered, as are exactly parallel with the disposition we have made of them in this book; not, that is not intended, but we must retain in our memories these general precepts of civility that thereby we may be enabled to pay every man his due respect upon all occasions, and do all things according to our own choice and discretion. For instance, if we are obliged to be civil to persons of quality, we are obliged, *a fortiori*, to be so to princes; and if to princes, much more to crowned heads or their ministers. In short, civility is not only to be uniform, but paid with discretion.

This also is to be observed in the practice of civility, we are much subject to fall into two dangerous extremes.

The first is, when we exceed in our civilities, heaping our impertinent discourse upon the person we would court, and admiring him in everything; this part of civility is no other but flattery, which is usually cast out as a lure, to bring down the grandee to some designs of our own; and this flattery does equally redound to both their advantages. For as he that is the parasite discovers a false object and interested soul; so he that is flattered and swallows it, shows his judgment and penetration to be but weak, to suffer himself to be cajoled and affected with those formal adorations which are not founded in the least upon any consideration of his merit.

The other error (to which likewise we are frequently liable) is, when out of too much fear or curiosity we are scrupulous of everything, making ourselves slaves to these ceremonies, and by an immoderate desire of being exact, becoming troublesome and ridiculous to everybody.

Civility ought to be frank and natural, without any superstition, and hence it is, that having performed our formalities, and paid those respects a person of quality might in reason expect, we are not afterwards to show any awe, or timorousness before him, but speak freely and ingeniously to him; for that diffidence or awe is many times troublesome even to the person we discourse with, and implied but mean education.

Which [this] makes it evident (contrary to the opinion of most people) that to be modest and civil is not to be pusillanimous or poor spirited, nor depresses nor obscures such as do use it; but being a restraint to that audacity and shamelessness which renders us unacceptable to all persons of discretion. We must confess that maxim of Cicero's to be very true that without modesty nothing can be laudable, without modesty nothing can be civil.

ı Sine verecundia nihil rectum effc nihil rectum.

A bashful man is not his own master, nor uses his own judgment, but is over awed by the boldness of others, and they that are impudent have a power over him. It is an evil guardian to youth, betraying it contrary to its own desire and inclination to the worst of men, who hurry them to evil actions and places. How many men have lost their estates, honors, and lives because they are ashamed to distrust? A man invites you to game, drink, rob, to be bound for him; this foolish modesty is to be cast off, deny him. An impudent flatterer comes to eat upon you, he begs a horse, a ring, a garment of you, give to the deserver. Respect him not that begs. Some are so bashful as not to send for a good physician, nor employ a good lawyer nor governor, because they are acquainted with a worse.

Begin betimes to break this fault, and in small matters assert your own liberty, deny to debauch, deny to lend money, or to admire everyone you hear praised; be constant, and be not overcome by importunity, which is a part of impudence, and is only becoming to them that want, and is in opposition to what we call mealy mouthed.

Chapter 19
Some General Observations to Remember in Regulating Actions

It is natural to all mankind to love and to desire to be beloved, as the prime method to obtain other benefits and ensuing advantages that we aim at. To acquire this from others depends principally upon the behavior of ourselves. A man that would make himself beloved must first render himself amiable. Now this is done by behaving of ourselves civilly, or with civility to all men. Civility does chiefly consist in these three parts. 1. In not expressing by actions or speeches any injury, disesteem, or offence, or undervaluing of another. 2. In being ready to do all good offices and ordinary kindnesses for another; and 3. In receiving no injuries nor offences from others. That is in not resenting every word or action which may (perhaps rationally) be interpreted to disesteem or undervaluing. For our outward behavior in general, that is best that declares sincerity and uprightness of the heart. Every man is loved for his honesty, and villains pretend to it, and under that color practice deceit, a formal starched behavior is odious, and being forced and unnatural, clouds and despairs the soul.

Comity and affability are the ornaments of converse, and declare one a lover of mankind, and argue a good harmony and concord of the passions. They are made up of a mixture of civility and freedom, qualified with a respect to the person you converse with.

He that would be reckoned or esteemed in the place where he lives must be careful to perform all acts of justice in his dealing between man and man, according to the maxim. And above all things, let his word be as punctual as his bond, and as sacred even in the smallest matters. Nay, it should be more carefully observed than a bond; for herein his honor and honesty are the security. And this, though the cheapest policy, will secure his interest with all that know him; the want hereof makes one cheap, and censured by the meanest he converses with, and will render him suspected, when he intends the most heartily.

Honeſte vivere, neminem lædere, ſuum cuiq; tribuere. *Juſt. Inſt. cap. 1.*

Discover not the secret of a friend, it argues a shallow understanding, and a weakness. He that is not constant in preserving what is committed to him cannot be a friend. And such is a talkative man that uses his mouth like a sluice to let out all that is within him.

Say not to a man (that you have not more than common assurance of to be your bosom-friend) that you have a secret but dare not tell it. Neither press a man vehemently to conceal what you have imparted to him. It implies you suspect what you have done and distrust his prudence.

The vice or debauchery of another should never be the subject of public talk; not of your friend, because you love him; nor of your foe, because he is so; for this will be construed the hatred to the one, and in partiality to the other.

No man is to gain a reverence for his own vice, and he that vauntingly declares it, pulls off an outward, silken, glorious coat, to show a dirty, lousy shirt that is next to his skin. Every man's fault should be every man's secret; for he that divulges it is a scandal to them that hear him.

When you do a man a kindness, do it at first, rather than to let it by arguments or importunity be extorted from you. This is a double courtesy and wholly obliges the person to yourself.

If you have a debt upon you, which none almost can avoid, be punctual in your payments; and if possible, let not him that asks go without it; for by this means you probably either save his reputation, or capacitate him to a bargain to his advantage, and generally there is one of these at the bottom. For most men are unwilling to be troublesome to others but on constraint. He that neglects his debts is undone to the world and must not expect either to eat or sleep in peace, and a poor man's debt makes the greatest noise.

As a man should not let himself lie open to all the pumpings of the pragmatical (but put them off, and here droll is best), so to be over severe in not replying to ordinary and easy desires, and shy in giving his opinion in common demands, argues either pride or formality. The formal man tells you nothing but what is above the vulgar and obliges you with a favor which you must so look upon though the things often are not worth the keeping.

By this you may consider how far you may tell news, but tell none to him that pretends to be a statesman, nor ask him none; for the first he'll seem to slight, and seem to know it before; for the latter he thinks secrecy becomes him, and therefore you disoblige him.

When you represent the actions of any of your superiors, do it as candidly as you can. It is the method of the world for the lesser to depend upon the greater and if you aim at employment, avoid being censorious especially. Herein you may, before you are aware, cut that thread upon which your sole interest did depend.

Fancy and change lift most into employments, and there needs only on our part to stand in the way; and that man removes himself or his friends at a distance from him that comes too close with them in private.

If you are a favorite to a great man, aim not to have his ear solely to yourself; for his slips shall be sure to be imputed to you and what he does well to himself.

Let your diversions and your business be mixed together; for recreations, those of the body are better than those of the mind. They that can find themselves no employment, but their pleasures are in perpetual disease. It is as if a man should never eat any substantial meat but live only upon sauce. Surely no man should live in this world that has nothing to do in it.

Say not you are extremely busy, nor that you have such a great deal of business, but rather go about it and do it, and when it is done, you will be more esteemed.

Scorn not any man for the infirmities of nature, which art cannot amend nor hide; nor delight to mention them since they often create envy, and sometimes, revenge.

Show not yourself joyful and pleased at the misfortunes that have befallen another, though you hated him. It argues a mischievous mind and that you had a desire to have done it yourself if you had had power or opportunity to you will.

These precepts are rather reducible to the rules of prudence than civility properly; but they two being so nearly related, I conceived it not amiss to give them. No man can be a civil man that is not a wise man; wherefore to conclude, I shall tell you what a wise man is. He hears rather than talks. [He] believes not easily, judges seldom, and then upon examination, [and] deliberates before he resolves.

174

[He] is constant in his resolutions, [and] fears not to repent. He speaks well of all; defends the fame of the absent, is courteous [but not] flattering, [and] readier to give than to receive. [He] loves his friends, but does nothing unworthy for their sakes. [He] is ready to assist and pleasure all men, many times unknown. He considers events before they happen, and then is neither exalted to dejected. He will avoid anxiety and moroseness, is even in his carriage, [and] true in his words. [He is] the same in reality as he is in show, admires few, derides none, envies none, despises none, no not the most miserable. He delights in the company of wise and virtuous persons; proffers not his counsel when he understands not well; and is content with his condition. He does not anything through contention, emulation, or revenge, but endeavors to do good for evil. He labors to know so much as to be able to depend upon his own judgment, though he does not, etc. but let this suffice.

Chapter 20
The Conclusion

This, sir, is all I am able to answer to your demands. I have already declared my opinion that it is impossible to give precepts of civility for all sorts of occurrences. I am sensible. Also I have inserted several things, which being treated of by others, and known already to most people, may seem super-vacaneous, but it could not be otherwise; for being to discourse of the civility of men's actions which for the most part have been always the same (as what age is it from the beginning of the world to this day in which men have not eaten, drunk, spit, etc.), I cannot see how I could avoid making use of the same rules, our actions being the same; and therefore, civility being nothing but what reason upon the principles of nature and custom has established as convenient, there have been other people endued with reason as well as we, and by consequence as able to find out and deport themselves according to that convenience.

But for as much as it is probable, so many worthy persons as profess the instituting of youth, and have applied themselves very studiously thereunto, could not forget to propose to their pupils certain directions and rules of civility, that being one of the most necessary parts of instruction, at least, that which is most conspicuous and liable to the eyes of the world, could not but be civil and courteous themselves. We have reason therefore to hope, if you think fit, to communicate this treatise. The reader will not take it amiss if we have presumed to imitate them in some things.

In effect, to take things rigorously and in strictness, as they and we both are in this case; like those who compile laws which they never composed, and would doubtless make themselves ridiculous, should they pretend to merit thereby. So it is not to be taken in ill part, if others add their labor to ours, so they do not arrogate, or pretend to anything which belongs to another. In this manner I should think myself very happy if others taking their light from me should polish what I have only rough drawn. I say roughly drawn for he who at once should propose to himself to run through all the actions of man to which rules of civility might be applied would engage himself in a thing he would find to be impossible.

So then, though those who have written before us upon this subject of civility may have said very much if they have answered the copiousness of the matter; and we possibly have added something in this treatise to what they have said, yet I am assured many things have escaped us all, and remain to be found out by those who come after.

Moreover, that custom of which we have spoken is not so constant, but it permits innovation and frequent alteration of its laws; and no question but time will have the same influence upon our present as it has had upon former proceedings.

Heretofore, for example, one might, without incivility, have hawked and spit upon the ground before a person of quality, provided he put his foot upon it when he had done, now it is perfect clownishness and intolerable.

Formerly one might gape and yawn, and it was well enough if he did not talk while he was yawning. Now it is intolerable.

Not long since it was not absurd to dip his bread in the sauce if he had not gnawed it before. Now it is ill breeding.

In past times we had liberty to pull what we could not get down out of our mouths and throw it upon the ground, so we did it dexterously without being seen. Now it is nasty and insufferable.

Certain it is then, that custom can introduce, abolish, or alter our rules as she pleases. Yet civility arising essentially out of modesty, and modesty out of humility (which like the other virtues are founded upon unmoveable principles) it is constant and clear that though custom may, yet civility in its foundation can never change; for there will always be civility while there is modesty, and modesty while any humility is to be found.

FINIS

Glossary

A

Admiration: the act of admiring, wondering, etc.

Admire: to look upon with wonder, to be surprised at.

Affectation: an eager desire [to impress]; affectedness, formality, niceness, preciseness.

B

Base: low, mean, vile; cowardly, dishonest; close-fisted, stingy.

Becomingness: decency, suitableness either of dress, gesture or manners.

C

Carriage: behavior.

Ceremony: the outward part of religion or worship; a sacred rite or ordinance.

Chamber: an apartment or room in a house.

Civil: courteous, kind, well-bred. Also political, belonging to the citizens, city, or state.

Civility: courtesy, obligingness.

Clown: [from the Latin *colonus:* a farmer] a country-fellow; also an unmannerly person.

To Comport: to agree, to behave one's self.

Comportment: behavior.

Congee: a low bow or reverence.

Conscience: the opinion or judgment which the rational soul passes upon all one's actions; or the testimony or witness of one's own mind.

Conversation: discourse among persons, behavior, society.

Countenance: looks, face, visage; encouragement.

Curse: to wish ill to.

D

Demeanor: behavior.

Deportment: behavior, carriage.

Detract: to take from, to abate or lessen, to speak ill of, or slander.

Dignity: honor, reputation, advancement, some considerable preferment or employment.

Dignity: *Ecclesiastical,* is defined by *canonists,* to be an administration joined with some power and jurisdiction.

Discreet: wise, considerate, sober.

Divertissement: diversion, recreation, sport, pastime.

Docibility: docility; teachableness, apt to learn; tractableness.

E

Eminent: excellent, high, great, renowned.

F

To Father a thing upon a person: to impute it to him.

To Fisk: to run about hastily and heedlessly, flirting from place to place.

To Flirt: to banter or jeer. [Judging from the use of this word in combination with other words, it also means to tease as we think of a flirt, but with a more sexual connotation.]

A Fret: a fume, or heat of passion.

To Fret: to gnaw, (anger, as it is severe, gnaws at the heart); to be vexed or chafe in mind.

Frivolous: of no account or value, vain, slight, trifling, silly, foolish.

Froward: peevish, fretful, surly.

G

Grave: having a composed countenance, serious.

Great (Men): the Laity of the higher House of Parliament, and also the Knights of the lower House.

Guggle (guggling): to make a noise as a narrow-mouthed bottle does while it is emptying.

I

Immodesty: wantonness, unmannerliness.

Imperfection: the want of something that is requisite or suitable to the nature of a thing; unperfectness, defect.

To Impute: to attribute, account, reckon, or ascribe to.

To Indispose: to make unfit or uncapable.

Inferior: persons of lower rank or degree.

Infirmity: sickness, weakness, feebleness.

J

Just: righteous, reasonable, fit.

L

Leveret: a young hare, especially one in its first year.

Loll: to loll out the tongue - to let it hang out of the mouth.

Lusty: strong in body, healthful.

M

Manfulness: valor, stoutness.

Malice: ill-will, grudge, or spite.

Mean: common, vulgar; low, poor, indifferent, pitiful.

Megrim: a distemper causing great pain in the temples and forepart of the head.

Modest: sober, grave, discreet in behavior.

O

Obstinate: willful, resolute, stubborn.

Order (orderly): a disposing of things in their proper place, rule or discipline.

P

Peevish: fretful.

Pensive: sad, heavy, sorrowful, thoughtful.

Pet: a distaste.

Take Pet: to be offended, to snuff at, to be angry.

Play: to divert by play. To play: divertissement (definition above).

Poltering (to polt): to beat back or thresh.

Prattle: to talk or chat as children do. Hieroglyphically a prattler is represented by a grasshopper because it is never quiet in summer, but fills the air with its importunate singing.

Prefer: to esteem above, or set more by; to advance or promote; to bring in, in speaking of a Bill, Indictment, or Law.

Q

Quality: condition, nature, inclination, habit; also title of honor, noble, birth.

R

Reprehend: to reprove or rebuke.

Reprobate: very wicked or lewd; cast out of favor; rejected.

Reproach: to upbraid, disgrace, shame.

Reverence: to honor or respect; submissive carriage towards superiors; also a congee or bow in token of respect.

Revile: to reproach, to taunt or rail at.

S

Salute: (noun) an outward mark of civility, a bow or a congee.

Settledness: a fixedness, of being settled in place, mind, etc.

Shamefaced: modest or bashful.

Sober: moderate, temperate, modest, grave, serious.

Sobriety: prudent and grave carriage; temperance and moderation in eating, drinking, etc.

Stout: lusty, hard, bold, courageous.

Superfluous: over-abundance, more than necessary, unnecessary, idle, needless, unprofitable.

Superior: one who is above others in authority, etc.; our betters, governors, magistrates, etc.

Surly: morose, sour, surly, sullen, stubborn.

T

Tedious: over-long, long-winded, irksome, wearisome.

Tractable: that may be handled, easily managed or ordered; flexible, gentle.

To Treat: to handle or discourse of a subject; to entertain; to be upon a treaty or bargain; to compound for a debt.

Troublesome: troubling, perplexing, disturbing, etc.

Troublesomeness: a troublesome quality, nature, or faculty.

Troublous: troublesome, perplexing, or difficult.

Troublousness: disturbedness, perplexedness, etc.

U

Unbecoming: lacking decency and suitableness, either of dress, gesture, or manners.

Upbraid: to reproach, to revile.

V

Vermin: any kind of hurtful creatures or insects; as rats, mice, lice, fleas, bugs, etc.

Virtue: efficacy, power, force, quality, property.

Made in the USA
Monee, IL
04 November 2022

17132216R00105